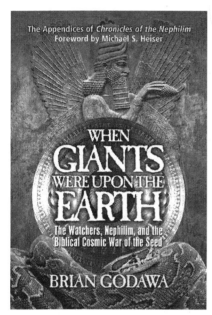

God Against the gods
Storytelling, Imagination
& Apologetics in the Bible

By Brian Godawa

God Against the gods: Storytelling, Imagination And Apologetics In The Bible
1st Edition

Embedded Pictures Publishing
Los Angeles, CA
brian@godawa.com
www.godawa.com

ISBN: 978-1-942858-18-8 (Paperback)
ISBN: 978-1-942858-19-5 (Kindle)

Scripture quotations taken from *The Holy Bible: English Standard Version.* Wheaton: Standard Bible Society, 2001.

Table of Contents

This book was previously released under the title: *Myth Became Fact: Storytelling, Apologetics and Imagination in the Bible*. A new chapter has been added. It is a compilation of various published articles and book appendices by Brian Godawa.

Special thanks to my editor, Don Enevoldsen.

PREFACE

Of Myth and the Bible

Whenever I consider that I have something important to say about faith, imagination, and/or apologetics, I usually discover that C.S. Lewis has already said it long before I could, and he has said it better than I will. True to form, his famous essay, *Myth Became Fact*, describes the heart of Christianity as a myth that is also a fact. He comforts the fearful modernist Christian whose faith in the Bible as a book of doctrine and abstract propositions is suddenly upset by the frightful reality of the interaction of holy writ with legend, pagan parallels, and mythology.

Rather than deny the ancient mythopoeic nature of God's Word as modern Evangelicals tend to do, Lewis embraced it as a reflection of God's preferred choice of concrete communication over abstraction (the worshipped discourse of the modernist). He understood myth to be the truth embedded into the creation by the Creator in such a way that even pagans would reflect some elements of that truth. Thus, when God Himself incarnates truth into history in the life, death, and resurrection of Jesus Christ, it is no surprise that it takes on mythopoeic dimensions reflected in previous pagan notions of dying and rising gods.

He concludes his essay with these memorable words:

> We must not be ashamed of the mythical radiance resting on our theology. We must not be nervous about "parallels" and "pagan Christs" — they ought to be there — it would be a stumbling block if they weren't. We must not, in false spirituality, withhold our imaginative welcome. If God chooses to be mythopoeic — and is not the sky itself a myth — shall we refuse to be mythopathic? For this is the marriage of heaven and earth: perfect myth and perfect fact: claiming not only our love and our obedience, but also our wonder and delight, addressed to the savage, the child, and

the poet in each one of us no less than to the moralist, the scholar, and the philosopher.[1]

A common reaction of many Christians to the word *myth* is often one of mistrust. In their minds, "myth" means "false," and since the Word of God can never be false, the category of myth is anathema in relation to the Bible.

But this is not an accurate assessment of the varied understandings of myth. Because of a modernist bias of anti-supernaturalism, some scholars define myth as "a necessary and universal form of expression within the early stage of man's intellectual development, in which unexplainable events were attributed to the direct intervention of the gods."[2] In some critical and liberal quarters of theology, this connotation has stuck to the meaning of myth and certainly warrants critique in light of its prejudicial definition that assumes a materialist universe without supernatural agents.

But a more specific and recent definition of myth is appropriate to our discussion. In this sense, myths are, as Northrop Frye has explained, "stories that tell a society what is important for it to know, whether about its gods, its history, its laws, or its structures."[3] In this sense, mythical stories, whether historically factual or fictional, do the same thing; they reveal true transcendent meaning. By this definition, calling the Bible mythical in some of its characteristics or imagery is not to jeopardize its historical claims. In fact, the Bible often claims to reveal the unseen transcendent meaning and purposes behind immanent historical events. Thus, Lewis' phrase, "myth became fact."

The problem comes when Christians seek to protect the Bible's reliability by demanding it be "historical" or "factually accurate" according to modern definitions of history writing and factual reporting or observation. They conclude that if the Bible is not accurate according to the "plain reading" of the text, then it cannot be relied upon to be truthful about the more important issues of God and salvation.

---

[1] C.S. Lewis, *God in the Dock*, (Fount Publishing, 1998, 1970), 67.
[2] Brevard S. Childs, *A Study of Myth in Genesis 1-11*, (Dissertation, zur Erlangung der Doktorwurde der Theologischen Fakultat der Universitat Basel, 1955), 1-2.
[3] Robert A. Armour, *Gods and Myths of Ancient Egypt* (Cairo, Egypt and New York, NY: The American University in Cairo Press, 2001), 2.

Let the reader be careful to note that I did not deny the historicity of the Bible, but I did make a distinction between *our modern notion* of what constitutes historical writing (historiography) and the ancient's notion of what constituted historical writing. For us to demand that the Biblical text be scientifically or historically "accurate" *as we define those terms* is not a high view of Scripture, it is a low view of Scripture. It is in fact imposing our own prejudices upon the text by refusing to understand it within its context. This is called cultural imperialism and it is the height of hubris, or human pride.

One example of this kind of modern hubris in defining history can be found in the notion of genealogies. In the Bible, genealogies are often used as apologetic tools to prove chosen lineage. The modern notion of historical precision and chronological accuracy is not always a part of the Biblical understanding of genealogy that prioritizes theological truth over historical veracity. The genealogical formula of Genesis, "X is the son of Y" that once was interpreted as the "plain reading" of literal sons is now universally acknowledged to involve historical gaps which renders the term "son of" as often figurative and not literal. "X is the son of Y" often means, "X is a descendent of Y." This is not liberal denigration of the Bible, it is the Bible's own context of meaning when it comes to genealogies.

The most important genealogy to Christians is of course that of Jesus Christ, the Son of God and "Son of David." In Matthew chapter 1, Matthew details Christ's genealogy and concludes, "So all the generations from Abraham to David were fourteen generations, and from David to the deportation to Babylon fourteen generations, and from the deportation to Babylon to the Christ fourteen generations" (1:17). So Matthew uses Christ's genealogy as an apologetic by exegeting the symbolic number of 14 as being historically symmetrical in the lineage. There's only one problem: It's not historically accurate — at least by *our* definition of history. And it is the Bible itself that proves this, not liberal theology.

As Bible commentator Craig Blomberg explains,

> The actual number of generations in the three parts to the genealogy are thirteen, fourteen, and thirteen, respectively...
> When one compares the genealogy with Luke's account (Luke 3:23–37) and with various Old Testament narratives,

3

it is clear that Matthew has omitted several names to achieve this literary symmetry.[4]

The Bible itself shows us that Biblical genealogies are not always historically accurate by our modern definitions of history. They are first and foremost theological in their interpretation and only secondarily are they historical. So to suggest that the way the Bible treats history sometimes includes figurative or mythopoeic dimensions that are not scientifically precise by our reckoning is not liberal subterfuge but Biblical fidelity. It is an unbiblical and humanistic belief to assume that the understanding of the Bible's approach to historical writing matches our understanding of historical writing. I hope to show in this book that there are quite a few more elements of mythopoeia and imagination that God uses that may make the modern Christian uncomfortable, but are clearly Biblical.

My approach in this book is to understand the Bible in its own ancient Near Eastern context, and thereby subordinate my own perspective to the perspective of the original writers and readers to whom the text was given. I seek to let the Bible define how it does history, fact, and imagination, and then I submit to that Biblical authority in how I seek to understand its meaning. The Bible is my authority, I am not the authority over the Bible.

To liberal theologians and critical scholars, this is antiquated fundamentalism, and to actual fundamentalists, it is syncretism, the attempt to blend pagan myths with the Bible. But the argument I make in this book is that the truth is neither of these bigoted hermeneutics, or prejudiced interpretations. I believe that God is doing something much more creative than fundamentalist believers and fundamentalist critics realize.

I believe that the Bible is God's Word and as such, it is breathed out of God through the writings of men inspired by the Holy Spirit. So, while the Biblical writers are very human and therefore very much creatures of their time and culture, there is also another author who is operating providentially behind the writing of the text to communicate transcendent truth, and that is the author and finisher of our faith, God Himself.

---

[4] Craig Blomberg, vol. 22, *Matthew*, *The New American Commentary*, 53 (Nashville: Broadman & Holman Publishers, 1992).

How He actually does this, I do not know, but the divine authorship does not reduce the human authorship to dictation or automatic writing. God uses the genre conventions and mindset of the ancient time period within which to communicate His transcendent truth.

This is what is called "accommodation" by theologians. In the same way that Jesus Christ is God incarnate within human flesh, so the Scriptures are God's message incarnate within human writings of the ancient Jewish world. A major part of that Jewish worldview was the special calling of a nation out of the nations of the earth to be His own people. God does separate Himself from the gods of the pagans, but at the same time, he utilizes much of the mythopoeic imagination that Israel shared with its pagan neighbors to communicate that separation.

One of the complaints of Christian apologists about the use of imagination and poetics in articulating or defending the faith is that it tends to lack the clarity of logical argumentation and rational discourse. The fuzziness and ambiguity of images, stories, metaphors and symbols tend to obscure or dilute the message of the Gospel. My book *Word Pictures: Knowing God Through Story and Imagination* deconstructs this rationalistic modernist fallacy as unbiblical. God uses so much imagery, symbolism, metaphor and poetic figurative language throughout the Scriptures (about 80% of the Bible) that one could even say he prefers it to abstract logical propositions (about 20% of the Bible).

Jesus is famous — or should I say *infamous* — for using parables to teach about the Kingdom of God instead of rational sermons of doctrinal exposition. Ironically, He quotes the Old Testament as explanation for why He used such fuzzy ambiguity in His parables:

> Matthew 13:10–17
> Then the disciples came and said to Him, "Why do you speak to them in parables?" And He answered them, "To you it has been given to know the secrets of the kingdom of heaven, but to them it has not been given. For to the one who has, more will be given, and he will have an abundance, but from the one who has not, even what he has will be taken away. This is why I speak to them in parables, because

seeing they do not see, and hearing they do not hear, nor do they understand. Indeed, in their case the prophecy of Isaiah is fulfilled that says:

"'You will indeed hear but never understand,
and you will indeed see but never perceive."
For this people's heart has grown dull,
and with their ears they can barely hear,
and their eyes they have closed,
lest they should see with their eyes
and hear with their ears
and understand with their heart
and turn, and I would heal them.'

But blessed are your eyes, for they see, and your ears, for they hear. For truly, I say to you, many prophets and righteous people longed to see what you see, and did not see it, and to hear what you hear, and did not hear it."

The use of parables by Jesus had the two-fold purpose of revealing the truth only to those who "have ears to hear," and concealing from those who were unrepentant in rejecting the Gospel. One could say that Jesus engaged in an anti-apologetic apologetic. That is, He embedded the truth into imagination in order to avoid the inevitable confrontation of debaters who were more interested in arguing than in discerning truth. Only those who wanted truth would recognize it in the imaginative form the parables incarnated. A Master storyteller may have a deeper influence on culture than a Masters in Apologetics.

Now, I don't want to appear to be an anti-intellectual who scorns the use of traditional apologetics. I have aggressively argued for a proper place of rational argumentation in *Word Pictures*. My real goal is to uncover the *unreasonable exaltation* of modernist rational abstraction and empirical observation when it comes to articulation and defense of the Gospel.

But I also want to provide a positive case for the Biblical use of the equally important imagination and storytelling. And yes, that means I am writing a book that engages in rational argumentation for the Biblical use of imagination in theology and apologetics. I do this because I maintain an ultimate equivalency between reason and imagination when it comes to truth. If you want to read examples of actual application of imagination, watch the movies I've written and read my novel series *Chronicles of the Nephilim, Chronicles of the Watchers* and *Chronicles of the Apocalypse* (www.godawa.com). I am a both/and writer on this issue, not an either/or curmudgeon.

In the spirit of this both/and approach, I offer this volume to explore the following essays that address storytelling, imagination, and apologetics in the Bible:

In Chapter One, "Demonizing the Pagan Gods," I lay out the basic premise of this entire book, that God does in fact demonize his opponents and their beliefs, both human and divine, by showing the demonic reality behind their earthly façade. We wrestle not against flesh and blood, so our polemics should take that into account.

In Chapter Two, "Old Testament Storytelling Apologetics," I address two mythopoeic elements that Israel shared with other ancient Near Eastern peoples, the sea dragon of chaos, and the storm god. These are polemical concepts that are used by Biblical writers to show Yahweh as incomparably superior to the gods of Canaan.

In Chapter Three, "Biblical Creation and Storytelling," I tease out the genre of creation stories in the ancient Near East and the Bible, which express a primeval battle called *Chaoskampf*, as well as a symbol of covenant establishment that is defined in *both* comparison *and* contrast with surrounding pagan nations.

In Chapter Four, "The Universe in Ancient Imagination," I do a detailed study of the Biblical picture of the universe as being very similar to the ancient Mesopotamian one, and alien to our own. I explain how this shows God's real intent behind His description of the universe as one of theological meaning and not physical description. This is a case of God using common understanding in order to communicate His transcendent superiority through finite writers of His message.

In Chapter Five, "New Testament Storytelling Apologetics," I exegete Paul's sermon to the pagans on Mars Hill as an example of communicating the Gospel in terms of the Stoic narrative with a view toward subverting their worldview.

In Chapter Six, "Imagination in Prophecy and Apocalypse," I examine some of the mythopoeic imagery used by God to deliberately obscure His message to unbelievers while simultaneously "proving" to believers his claim about the true meaning and purpose behind history.

Chapter Seven, "An Apologetic of Biblical Horror," explores the otherwise offensive genre of horror writing to show how God Himself uses it as a powerful moral tool to communicate serious spiritual, moral, and social defilement in the context of repentance from sin and redemptive victory over evil.

While this is a collection of essays from assorted books and articles I have written, the unifying thread that connects them all is an underlying theme of Gods' use of storytelling and imagination as an apologetic tool in the Bible. My hope is that the Christian reader may gain inspiration from these insights to begin using more imagination in their own approach to communicating and defending the faith and glorifying God, since it is a severely underappreciated element of God's word.

CHAPTER 1

Demonizing the Pagan Gods

This chapter expands upon some material from my scholarly book, "When Giants Were Upon the Earth."

In American political and religious discourse, the act of "demonizing" one's opponents is considered insulting, something that discredits one's arguments. It charges that the "demonizer" is the one at fault for casting "the other" or their ideas with dishonest exaggeration. It's based on the assumption that such extremes of evil do not exist in human beings or their ideas. It assumes that demons do not exist.

But what if demons do exist? What if someone or their ideas really are demonic or truly evil? Then demonization is not a moral fallacy, but a morally appropriate act of designation. In that case, we *ought* to demonize the truly demonic.

It might surprise those self-assured indoctrinated Americans to discover that God himself demonizes his opponents, the pagan gods of the ancient world and their ideas with them.

Demonic Ideas

To start with, the apostles in the New Testament vigorously affirm that some ideas are so evil, they qualify as "demonic." The apostle Paul calls the forbidding of marriage and the forced abstinence from certain foods for religious reasons "teaching of demons" and "deceitful spirits," or, as I prefer with this older English translation, "doctrines of devils" (1 Tim. 4:1).

The apostle James describes bitterness, jealousy, selfish ambition and boasting as being "demonic wisdom that does not come down from above, but is earthly and unspiritual." (James 3:13).

What these apostles are demonizing are not the explicitly spiritual teachings of necromancers, sorcerers and other spiritualists. They are not referring to the ontological reality of evil spirits, but rather to the moral behavior and religious teachings of people in their own fold! This is not a debate about whether one can lose their salvation. Paul was speaking of the Judaizers, those who claimed that in order to be a Christian, you must also follow the law of Torah. James was talking about those in the Christian congregation who were jockeying for power and causing division.

So much for the stigma of demonization. There are some ideas and behaviors that are so evil in their spiritual implications, they deserve to be called out as demonic.

The Gods as Demons

But that was only a warm-up. Because God also demonizes individuals and the pagan gods they worship – in both Old and New Testaments.

The Old Testament. A common understanding of absolute monotheism is that when the Bible refers to other gods it does not mean that the gods are real beings but merely *beliefs* in real beings that do not exist. For instance, when Deuteronomy 32:43 proclaims "rejoice with him, O heavens, bow down to him, all gods," this is a poetic way of saying "what you believe are gods are not gods at all because Yahweh is the only God that exists." What seems to support this interpretation is the fact that a few verses before this (v. 39), God says, "See now, that I, even I am he, and there is no god [elohim] beside me." Does this not clearly indicate that God is the only God [elohim] that really exists out of all the "gods" [elohim] that others believe in?

Not in its Biblical context it doesn't.

When the text is examined in its full context of the chapter and the rest of the Bible we discover a very different notion about God and gods. The phrase "I am, and there is none beside me" was an ancient Biblical slogan of incomparability of sovereignty, not exclusivity of existence. It was a way of saying that a certain authority was the most powerful *compared to* all other authorities. It did not mean that there were no other authorities that existed.

We see this sloganeering in two distinct passages, one of the ruling power of Babylon claiming proudly in her heart, "I am, and there is no one beside me" (Isa. 47:8), and the other of the city of Nineveh boasting in her heart, "I am, and there is no one else" (Zeph. 2:15). The powers of Babylon and Nineveh are obviously not saying that there are no other powers or cities that exist beside them, because they had to conquer other cities and rule over them. In the same way, Yahweh uses that colloquial phrase, not to deny the existence of other gods, but to express his incomparable sovereignty over them.[1]

In concert with this phrase is the key reference to gods early in Deuteronomy 32. Israel is chastised for falling away from Yahweh after he gave Israel the Promised Land:

> Deut. 32:17
> They sacrificed to <u>demons</u> not God, to <u>gods</u> they had never known, to new gods that had come recently, whom your fathers had never dreaded.

In this key text we learn that the idols or gods of the other nations that Israel worshipped were real beings that existed called "demons" (Hebrew: *shedim*). At the same time, they are called, "gods" and "not God," which indicates that they exist as real gods, but are not THE God of Israel.

Psalm 106 repeats this same exact theme of Israel worshipping the gods of other nations and making sacrifices to those gods that were in fact demonic.

> Psa. 106:34-37
> They did not destroy the peoples, as the LORD commanded them, but they <u>mixed with the nations</u> and learned to do as they did. They served their <u>idols</u>, which became a snare to them. They sacrificed their sons and their daughters to the <u>demons</u>.

---

[1] Michael S. Heiser, "Monotheism, Polytheism, Monolatry, or Henotheism? Toward an Assessment of Divine Plurality in the Hebrew Bible" (2008). Faculty Publications and Presentations. Paper 277, p. 12-15, http://digitalcommons.liberty.edu/cgi/viewcontent.cgi?article=1276&context=lts_fac_pubs&s ei-redir=1#search=%22heiser+Monotheism,+Polytheism,+Monolatry,+or+Henotheism%22 accessed March 23, 2011.

One rendering of the Septuagint (LXX) version of Psalm 95:5-6 reaffirms this reality of national gods being demons whose deity was less than the Creator, "For great is the Lord, and praiseworthy exceedingly. More awesome he is than all the gods. For all the gods of the nations are demons, but the Lord made the heavens."[2] Another LXX verse, Isa. 65:11, speaks of Israel's idolatry: "But ye are they that have left me, and forget my holy mountain, and prepare a table for [a demon], and fill up the drink-offering to Fortune [a foreign goddess]."[3]

In the Old Testament, Yahweh calls pagan gods what they really are: demons. He demonizes his opponents righteously. But this doesn't end with the Old Testament. The New Testament takes up the task as well.

The New Testament. In Revelation, the Apostle John defines the worship of gold and silver idols as being the worship of demons. The physical objects were certainly without deity as they could not "see or hear or walk," but the gods behind those objects were real beings with evil intent.

> Revelation 9:20
> The rest of mankind, who were not killed by these plagues, did not repent of the works of their hands nor give up worshiping demons and idols of gold and silver and bronze and stone and wood, which cannot see or hear or walk.

This is precisely the nuanced distinction that the Apostle Paul refers to when he addresses the issue of food sacrificed to idols—that is, physical images of deities on earth. He considers idols as having "no real existence," but then refers to other "gods" in the heavens or on earth *who do exist*, but are *not the same* as the One Creator God:

---

[2] Randall Tan, David A. deSilva, and Logos Bible Software. *The Lexham Greek-English Interlinear Septuagint*. Logos Bible Software, 2009. Baruch 4:7 in the Apocrypha echoes this Scriptural theme as well when speaking of Israel's apostasy: "For you provoked him who made you, by sacrificing to demons and not to God."

[3] Lancelot Charles Lee Brenton, *The Septuagint Version of the Old Testament: English Translation* (London: Samuel Bagster and Sons, 1870), Is 65:11. Randall Tan and David A. deSilva, Logos Bible Software, *The Lexham Greek-English Interlinear Septuagint* (Logos Bible Software, 2009), Is 65:11.

1 Cor. 8:4-6

Therefore, as to the eating of food offered to idols, we know that "an idol has no real existence," and that "there is no God but one." For although there may be so-called gods in heaven or on earth—as indeed there are many "gods" and many "lords"—yet for us there is one God, the Father, from whom are all things and for whom we exist, and one Lord, Jesus Christ, through whom are all things and through whom we exist.

1 Cor. 10:18-20

Consider the people of Israel: are not those who eat the sacrifices participants in the altar? What do I imply then? That food offered to idols is anything, or that an idol is anything? No, I imply that what pagans sacrifice they offer to demons and not to God. I do not want you to be participants with demons.

In 1 Corinthians, as in Revelation 9 quoted earlier, gods are not merely figments of imagination without existence in a world where the Trinity is the sole deity residing in the spiritual realm. Rather, physical idols (*images*) are "nothing," and "have no real existence" in that they are the representatives of the deities, not the deities themselves. But the deities behind those idols are real demonic beings; the gods of the nations who are not THE God, for they themselves were created by God and are therefore essentially incomparable to the God through whom we exist.

The terminology used by Paul in the first passage contrasting the many gods and lords with the one God and Lord of Christianity reflects the client-patron relationship that ANE cultures shared. As K.L. Noll explains in his text on ancient Canaan and Israel, "Lord" was the proper designation for a patron in a patron-client relationship. There may have been many gods, but for ancient Israel, there was only one Lord, and that was Yahweh."[4]

---

[4] K.L. Noll, *Canaan and Israel in Antiquity: An Introduction*, New York: NY; Shefffield Academic Press, 2001, p. 212.

Gods of the Nations

Returning to Deuteronomy 32 and going back a few more verses in context, we read of a reality-changing incident that occurred at Babel:

> Deut. 32:8-9
> When the Most High gave to the nations their inheritance, when he divided mankind, he fixed the borders of the peoples according to the number of the sons of God. But the LORD's portion is his people, Jacob his allotted heritage.

The reference to the creation of nations through the division of mankind and fixing of the borders of nations is clearly a reference to the event of the Tower of Babel in Genesis 11 and the dispersion of the peoples into the 70 nations listed in Genesis 10.

But then there is a strange reference to those nations being "fixed" according to the number of the sons of God.[5] We'll explain in a moment that those sons of God are from the assembly of the divine council of God. But after that, the text says that God saved Jacob (God's own people) for his "allotment." Even though Jacob was not born until long after the Babel incident, this is an anachronistic way of referring to what would become God's people, because right after Babel, we read about God's calling of Abraham who was the grandfather of Jacob (Isa. 41:8; Rom. 11:26). So God allots nations and their geographic territory to these sons of God to rule over as their inheritance, but he allots the people of Jacob to himself, along with their geographical territory of Canaan (Gen. 17:8).

The idea of Yahweh "allotting" geographical territories to these sons of God who really existed and were worshipped as gods (idols) shows up again in several places in Deuteronomy:

---

[5] The astute reader will notice that some Bible translations read "according to the sons of Israel." The ESV reflects the latest consensus of scholarship that the Septuagint (LXX) and the Dead Sea Scrolls (DSS) segment of this verse is the earlier and more accurate reading than the later Masoretic Text (MT) of the same. See Heiser, Michael, "Does Deuteronomy 32:17 Assume or Deny the Reality of Other Gods?" (2008). Faculty Publications and Presentations. Paper 322, p 137-145. http://digitalcommons.liberty.edu/lts_fac_pubs/322/

Deut. 4:19-20
And beware lest you raise your eyes to heaven, and when you see the sun and the moon and the stars, all the host of heaven, you be drawn away and bow down to them and serve them, things that the LORD your God has allotted to all the peoples under the whole heaven.

Deut. 29:26
They went and served other gods and worshiped them, gods whom they have not known and whom He had not allotted to them.

"Host of heaven" was a term that referred to astronomical bodies that were also considered to be gods or members of the divine council.[6] The *Encyclopedia Judaica* notes that, "in many cultures the sky, the sun, the moon, and the known planets were conceived as personal gods. These gods were responsible for all or some aspects of existence. Prayers were addressed to them, offerings were made to them, and their opinions on important matters were sought through divination."[7]

But it was not merely the pagans who made this connection of heavenly physical bodies with heavenly spiritual powers. The Old Testament itself equates the sun, moon, and stars with the angelic "sons of God" who surround God's throne, calling them both the "host of heaven" (Deut. 4:19; 32:8-9).[8] Jewish commentator Jeffrey Tigay writes, "[These passages] seem to reflect a Biblical view that... as punishment for man's repeated spurning of His authority in primordial times (Gen. 3-11), God deprived mankind at large of true knowledge of Himself and ordained that it should worship idols and subordinate celestial beings."[9]

---

[6] H. Niehr, "Host of Heaven," Toorn, K. van der, Bob Becking, and Pieter Willem van der Horst. *Dictionary of Deities and Demons in the Bible DDD*. 2nd extensively rev. ed. Leiden; Boston; Grand Rapids, Mich.: Brill; Eerdmans, 1999., 428-29; I. Zatelli, "Astrology and the Worship of the Stars in the Bible," *ZAW* 103 (1991): 86-99.

[7] "Astrology", *Encyclopaedia Judaica* Michael Berenbaum and Fred Skolnik, eds. 2nd ed. Detroit: Macmillan Reference USA, 2007, p. 8424.

[8] See also Deut 4:19; Deut 17:3; 2King 23:4-5; 1King 22:19; Neh 9:6.

[9] Jeffrey Tigay, *JPS Torah Commentary: Deuteronomy* (Philadelphia: The Jewish Publication Society, 1996): 435; as quoted in Michael S. Heiser, "Deuteronomy 32:8 and the Sons of God," *Bibliotheca Sacra* 158 (January-March 2001): 72; online: http://thedivinecouncil.com/.

There is more than just a symbolic connection between the physical heavens and the spiritual heavens in the Bible. In some passages, the stars of heaven are linked *interchangeably* with angelic heavenly beings, also referred to as "holy ones" or "sons of God" (Psa. 89:5-7; Job 1:6).[10]

Daniel 10:10-21 speaks of these divine "host of heaven" allotted with authority over pagan nations as spiritual "princes" or rulers battling with the archangels Gabriel and Michael.

> Daniel 10:13, 20
> [13] The prince of the kingdom of Persia withstood me twenty-one days, but Michael, one of the chief princes, came to help me... [20] "But now I will return to fight against the prince of Persia; and when I go out, behold, the prince of Greece will come.

In conclusion, the entire narrative of Deuteronomy 32 tells the story of God dispersing the nations at Babel and allotting the pagan nations to be ruled by "gods" who were demonic fallen divine beings. God then allots the people of Israel for himself, through Abraham, and their territory of Canaan. But God's people fall away from him and worship these other pagan gods and are judged for their apostasy.

We will now see that Yahweh will judge these gods as well.

Psalm 82

Bearing in mind this notion of Yahweh allotting gods over the Gentile nations while maintaining Canaan and Israel for himself, read this following important Psalm 82 where Yahweh now judges those gods for injustice and proclaims the Gospel that he will eventually take back the nations from those gods.

---

[10] See also Job 38:4-7; Neh. 9:6; Psa 148:2-3, 1King 22:29 & 2King 21:5. In Isa 14:12-14 the king of Babylon is likened to the planet Venus (Morningstar) seeking to reign above the other stars of heaven, which are equivalent to the sons of God who surround God's throne on the "mount of assembly" or "divine council" (see Psa 89:5-7 and Psa 82).

Psa. 82:1-8
God [elohim] has taken his place in the divine council;
in the midst of the gods [elohim] he holds judgment:
"How long will you judge unjustly
and show partiality to the wicked? *Selah*
Give justice to the weak and the fatherless;
maintain the right of the afflicted and the destitute.
Rescue the weak and the needy;
deliver them from the hand of the wicked."

They have neither knowledge nor understanding,
they walk about in darkness;
all the foundations of the earth are shaken.

I said, "You are gods [elohim]
sons of the Most High, all of you;
nevertheless, like men you shall die,
and fall like any prince."
Arise, O God, judge the earth;
for you shall inherit all the nations!

So from this text we see that God has a divine council that stands around him, and it consists of "gods" who are judging rulers over the nations and are also called *sons of the Most High* (synonymous with "sons of God"). Because they have not ruled justly, God will bring them low in judgment and take the nations away from them. Sound familiar? It's the same exact story as Deuteronomy 32:8-9 and Isaiah 24:21-22.

Isaiah 24:21–22
On that day the LORD will punish the host of heaven, in heaven, and the kings of the earth, on the earth. They will be gathered together as prisoners in a pit; they will be shut up in a prison, and after many days they will be punished.[11]

---

[11] Interestingly, this passage of Isaiah is not clear about what judgment in history it is referring to. But the language earlier in the text is similar to Psalm 82 and to the Flood when it

The idea that the Bible should talk about existent gods other than Yahweh is certainly uncomfortable for absolute monotheists. But our received definitions of monotheism are more often than not determined by our cultural traditions, many of which originate in theological controversies of other eras that create the baggage of non-Biblical agendas.

According to the Evangelical Protestant principle of *Sola Scriptura*, that the Bible alone is the final authority of doctrine, not tradition, believers are obligated to first find out what the Bible text says and then adjust their theology to be in line with Scripture, not the other way around. All too often we find individuals ignoring or redefining a Biblical text because it does not fit their preconceived notion of what the Bible *should* say, rather than what it actually says. The existence of other gods in Scripture is one of those issues.

In light of this theological fear, some try to reinterpret this reference of gods or sons of God as a poetic expression of human judges or rulers on earth metaphorically taking the place of God, the ultimate judge, by determining justice in his likeness and image. But there are three big reasons why this cannot be so: First, the terminology in the passage contradicts the notion of human judges and fails to connect that term ("sons of God") to human beings anywhere else in the Bible; Second, the Bible elsewhere explicitly reveals a divine council or assembly of supernatural sons of God that are judges over geographical allotments of nations that is more consistent with this passage; Third, a heavenly divine council of supernatural sons of God is more consistent with the ancient Near Eastern (ANE) worldview of the Biblical times that Israel shared with her neighbors.

What's in a Name

Another way in which God demonizes his opponents, the pagan gods, and their ideas is through name-calling. You read that right. I realize we think of name-calling as something immature children do on a playground.

---

says, "For the windows of heaven are opened, and the foundations of the earth tremble. 19 The earth is utterly broken, the earth is split apart, the earth is violently shaken. 20 The earth staggers like a drunken man; it sways like a hut; its transgression lies heavy upon it, and it falls, and will not rise again." So this may be another passage that uses a Flood reference tied in with the Watchers and their punishment.

But there is a reason why that is so prevalent, not merely amongst children, but through all of human history. Because the act of naming something is an act of authority over the object named. It's how God created us.

If you want to understand the nature of something, look at its origin. The origin of naming rooted in authority comes from Genesis 2. God created the Garden and placed Adam in it to tend it and keep it (Gen. 2:8, 15). Then he created the animals over which he would give man dominion and rule to subdue (Gen. 1:26-28). One expression of that dominion, or authority, was in the act of naming.

God brought the animals he created to the man "to see what he would call them. And whatever the man called every living creature, that was its name" (Gen. 2:19).

Ancient Near Eastern Biblical scholar, John Walton explains,

> Names are not given randomly in the ancient world. A name may identify the essential nature of the creature, so that giving a name may be an act of assigning the function that creature will have.
>
> In Mesopotamia the assigning of function is referred to as the decreeing of destiny. Decreeing destiny by giving a name is an act of authority. In the ancient world, when a king conquered another country, the king he put on the throne was given a new name. In other cases, the giving of a name is an act of discernment in which the name is determined by the circumstances. In either case, Adam's naming of the animals is his first step in subduing and ruling.[12]

The ancient world was patriarchal, that is, men were considered the authority over women in both society and marriage. While this may be offensive to the prejudices of our modern world, it was an organizing principle in the Bible. This is why the very next section of Genesis 2 shows

---

[12] John H Walton, Zondervan *Illustrated Bible Backgrounds Commentary (Old Testament): Genesis, Exodus, Leviticus, Numbers, Deuteronomy, vol. 1* (Grand Rapids, MI: Zondervan, 2009), 31–32.

Adam naming Eve, because he was the expressed authority over her. "She shall be called Woman, because she was taken out of Man" (Gen 2:23).

Since names were considered an incarnation of that person's essence or identity, or a change in their identity, God himself renames individuals for his purposes. We know that Abram's name which meant "exalted father" was changed to Abraham to mean "father of many nations" (Gen 17:5) based on the historical events of God's covenant with him. Later in the Bible, Jacob ("usurper") was changed to Israel ("struggles with God") as the ancestor of the people of God.

But God also renamed his enemies in the Bible. And often times, it was with mockery. Let's take a look at some of these demons.

Nimrod. Genesis 10:8-12 speaks of the mighty Nimrod, the first "warrior of name" after the Flood, who is credited with starting the kingdoms of Mesopotamia, including Babel, of the Tower of Babel infamy. The name of Nimrod is apparently a Hebrew play on words that demonized the leader, because Nimrod in Hebrew means "to revolt." One hardly thinks a person would make his name with such negative connotations, since such kings often considered themselves to be like the gods.

Scholars van der Toorn and van der Horst suggest that Nimrod was a deliberately distorted Hebrew version of Ninurta as the hunter god of Mesopotamia. They argue that the reign of Nimrod was most likely a symbolic synopsis of the history of Mesopotamia embodied in one character, a deity deliberately dethroned by the Jewish writer to a hunter king.

> The cities [of Nimrod] mentioned in Gen 10:9-12 are given in a more or less chronological sequence. The list reads as a condensed resume of Mesopotamian history. Akkad, though still in use as a cult-center in the first millennium, had its *floruit* under the Sargonic dynasty. Kalhu had its heyday in the first half of the first millennium BCE, some fifteen hundred years later. If Nimrod is not a god, he must at least

have enjoyed a divine longevity, his reign embracing both cities.[13]

To top off God's "verbal bullying" of the villainous Nimrod, the infamous city he began, was also renamed. *Babylon*, meaning "gateway of the gods," was renamed by the writer of Genesis to *Babel*, meaning "confusion of tongues." How's that for a sarcastic swipe at man's positive self-image?

Nimrod's name is an example where God mocks a foreign deified "god-king" and his arrogant kingdom by renaming him as a mere rebel and hunter.

Cushan-rishathaim. In Judges 3:8-9, this king of Mesopotamia is mentioned with hostility toward Israel. Though he is not a deity, and he is most likely Naram-Sin (2367-2359 B.C.), he is renamed in the text with insulting degradation. This snarky rename means "doubly wicked son of Cush."[14] Sometimes name-calling is appropriate when it comes to truly evil people.

Jezebel. In 2 Kings, we read the story of this most ruthless and wicked queen of Israel. She was a royal pagan from Tyre whom King Ahab of Israel married as a treaty of appeasement. It didn't work out well for Israel, as her idolatry infected Israel and brought judgment, in both physical and verbal condemnation. Archaeological discoveries have revealed that her name in Tyre was actually Izebul, which meant, "Where is the Prince?" *Prince* meaning, Ba'al, the prince of gods in Canaan. In the Bible, Izebul is named Jezebel, which is a slurring wordplay on the Hebrew word for "dung" (*zebel*). 2 Kings 9:37 reduces that worldly powerful queen to pathos with a double entendre of caustic scorn: "And the corpse of Jezebel shall be as dung on the face of the field in the territory of Jezreel, so that no one can say, 'This is Jezebel.'"

---

[13] K. van der Toorn and P. W. van der Horst, "Nimrod before and after the Bible," *Harvard Theological Review* 83 (1990): 1–29.
[14] Gerald E. Aardsma, Ph.D., *A New Approach to the Chronology of Biblical History from Abraham to Samuel* (Loda, IL: Aardsma Publishing, 2003, 2005), 76.

But God does not merely jab kings and rulers with his verbal flame throwing, he also mocks the gods by renaming them.

Ba'alzebub. Jezebel, that wicked queen of dung, had introduced Ba'al worship into Israel in an unprecedented way that would haunt the people of God for generations. Ba'al was a high god in Canaan and he took on many manifestations. In Ekron, his name was Ba'alzebul, which meant, "lord of the heavenly dwelling." The author of 2 Kings 1:2-6 renames Ba'alzebul as *Ba'alzebub*, which means the derogatory, "lord of the flies."[15] Ya gotta appreciate God's wicked sense of humor. Jesus carries on this tradition of mockery in the Gospels when he reduces that prince of gods to a prince of demons (Matt. 12:24 : Mark 3:22; Luke 11:15).

Ashtoreth. Ashtoreth is a goddess who shows up often in the Old Testament (1King 11:15, 33; 2King 23:13; 1Sam 31:10). The name refers to the infamous Ashtart (or Astarte) of Canaan. It is said that ignoring someone is the most vicious way to hurt them. False gods were bad enough to the ancient Hebrew, but female goddesses were so offensive that the Bible writers didn't use a word for goddess. They simply used their names. This may be because they believed that the demons behind the deities were of male gender, since angelic divine beings were all male. But it has long been noted that the name Ashtoreth was a deliberate diabolical distortion of Ashtart by using the vowels of the Hebrew word for "shame" (*bosheth*) between the consonants of Ashtart.[16]

Satyrs as Goat Demons

Another way of demonizing and mocking God's opponents was to use the pagan mythology against itself. That is, Biblical writers would quote or paraphrase pagan mythologies back to them, but in an undermining or ironic way. One of those examples is the references to satyrs in Biblical condemnation of false religion. Anyone familiar with ancient Greco-Roman

---

[15] "Baalzebub," *The International Standard Bible Encyclopedia, Revised.* (*ISBE*) Edited by Geoffrey W. Bromiley. Wm. B. Eerdmans, 1988.
[16] John Day, *Yahweh and the Gods and Goddesses of Canaan (The Library of Hebrew Bible/Old Testament Studies)* (Bloomsbury T&T Clark, 2002), 214.

religion has heard of Pan, the satyr deity of nature and shepherding. A satyr was a hybrid creature who had the upper body of a man, and the lower body and legs of a goat, accompanied by horns on his head as well. But these little nasties worshipped the chaos of unrestrained passion, in both sexual and consumptive behaviors. The notion of satyrs or goat deities finds a place in Canaanite lore, and therefore, in the Bible as well.

Take a look at these prophecies of Isaiah referencing the destruction of Edom and Babylon.

> Isaiah 34:11–15 (The destruction of Edom)
> [11]But the hawk and the porcupine shall possess it, the owl and the raven shall dwell in it... [13]Thorns shall grow over its strongholds, nettles and thistles in its fortresses. It shall be the haunt of jackals, an abode for ostriches. [14]And wild animals shall meet with hyenas; the wild goat (*seirim*) shall cry to his fellow.

> Isaiah 13:21–22 (The destruction of Babylon)
> [21]But wild animals will lie down there, and their houses will be full of howling creatures; there ostriches will dwell, and there wild goats (*seirim*) will dance. [22]Hyenas will cry in its towers, and jackals in the pleasant palaces; its time is close at hand and its days will not be prolonged.

The passages above speak of God's judgment upon the nations of Babylon and Edom (symbols of all that is against Israel and Yahweh). A cursory reading of the texts seem to indicate a common word picture of Yahweh destroying these nations so thoroughly that they end up a desert wasteland with wild animals and birds inhabiting them because the evil people will be no more.

Nothing about mythical monsters like satyrs there, right?

Wrong. Because the English translation of the Hebrew word *seirim* as "wild goats," obscures the full ancient meaning. If we look closer into the original Hebrew, we find a more expanded mythopoeic reference to pagan deities.

23

A look at the Septuagint (LXX) translation into Greek made by ancient Jews in the second century before Christ, reveals the hint of that different picture.

> Isaiah 34:13-14 (LXX)
> [11] and for a long time birds and hedgehogs, and ibises and ravens shall dwell in it: and the measuring line of desolation shall be cast over it, and <u>satyrs</u> shall dwell in it...[13] And thorns shall spring up in their cities, and in her strong holds: and they shall be habitations of <u>monsters,</u> and a court for ostriches. [14] And <u>devils shall meet with satyrs</u>, and they shall cry one to the other: <u>there shall satyrs rest,</u> having found for themselves *a place of* rest.[17]

> Isaiah 13:21-22 (LXX)
> But wild beasts shall rest there; and the houses shall be filled with howling; and <u>monsters</u> shall rest there, and devils shall dance there, [22] and <u>satyrs shall dwell there</u>.[18]

Wow, what a dramatic difference, huh? Of course, the LXX passages above are not in Greek, but are English translations, which adds a layer of complication that we will unravel shortly to reveal even more mythopoeic elements. But the point is made that ancient translators understood those words within their ancient context much differently than the modern bias of more recent interpreters.

The LXX translates the word for "satyrs" that appears in these Isaiah passages as *onokentaurois* or "donkey-centaurs," from which we get our word "centaur." The *Greek-English Lexicon of the Septuagint* defines this word as "donkey-centaur, mythic creature (a centaur resembling a donkey rather than a horse)."[19]

---

[17] Lancelot Charles Lee Brenton, *The Septuagint Version of the Old Testament: English Translation*, Is 34:13–14 (London: Samuel Bagster and Sons, 1870).

[18] Lancelot Charles Lee Brenton, *The Septuagint Version of the Old Testament: English Translation*, Is 13:21–22 (London: Samuel Bagster and Sons, 1870).

[19] Johan Lust, Erik Eynikel and Katrin Hauspie, *A Greek-English Lexicon of the Septuagint: Revised Edition* (Deutsche Bibelgesellschaft: Stuttgart, 2003).

In Isaiah 34:14 of the ESV we read of "the wild goat crying to his fellow," and in 13:21, "there wild goats will dance." But the underlying Hebrew (*seirim*) is not about wild goats, but satyrs, that were prevalent in Canaanite religion. Scholar Judd Burton points out that Banias or Panias at the base of Mount Hermon in Bashan was a key worship site for the Greek goat-god Pan as early as the third century B.C. and earlier connections to the goat-idol Azazel.[20]

Satyrs were well known for their satyrical dance, the *Sikinnis*, consisting of music, lascivious dance, licentious poetry and sarcastic critique of culture.[21] This reflects the mockery of the "goats" dancing on the ruins of Edom and Babylon in Isaiah.

The Bible writers considered the satyr deities to be demons and thus called them "goat demons." So prevalent and influential were these pagan gods that Yahweh would have trouble with Israel worshipping them as idols.

> Leviticus 17:7
> [7] So they shall no more sacrifice their sacrifices to <u>goat demons</u> (*seirim*), after whom they whore. This shall be a statute forever for them throughout their generations.

> 2 Chronicles 11:15
> [15] [Jeroboam] appointed his own priests for the high places and for the <u>goat idols</u> (*seirim*) and for the calves that he had made.

Not only did Israel fall into worshipping the *seirim* satyrs in Canaan, they were even committing spiritual adultery with them while in the wilderness! It is no wonder Yahweh considered them demons, a declaration reiterated in the Deuteronomy 32 worldview that after Israel would be

---

[20] Judd H. Burton, *Interview With the Giant: Ethnohistorical Notes on the Nephilim* (Burton Beyond Press, 2009) 19-21. "Regardless of his [Azazel's] origins—in pre-Israelite practice he was surely a true demon, perhaps a satyr, who ruled in the wilderness." Jacob Milgrom, *A Continental Commentary: Leviticus: a Book of Ritual and Ethics* (Minneapolis, MN: Fortress Press, 2004), 169.

[21] Gaston Vuillier, trans. Joseph Grego, *A History Of Dancing From The Earliest Ages To Our Own Times* (New York, NY: D. Appleton and Co., 1848), 27-28.

brought into Canaan by the hand of God, she would betray Yahweh by turning aside to other gods, redefined as demons.

The New Testament reiteration of this demon interpretation is in the Apostle John's inspired reuse of the *same exact language* from Isaiah when pronouncing judgment upon first century Israel as a symbolic "Mystery Babylon."

> Revelation 18:2
> [2]"Fallen, fallen is Babylon the great! She has become a dwelling place for demons, a haunt for every unclean spirit, a haunt for every unclean bird, a haunt for every unclean and detestable beast."[22]

Because of the exile under the Babylonians, Jews would use Babylon as the ultimate symbol of evil. So when John attacks his contemporaries in Israel for rejecting Messiah, he describes them as demonic Babylon worthy of the same judgment as that ultimate evil nation.

Lilith

Another pagan deity subverted in the Old Testament narrative is Lilith, the she-demon. Regarding this monster, the *Dictionary of Deities and Demons in the Bible* says its Mesopotamian narrative reaches back to the third millennium B.C.

> Here we find Inanna who plants a tree later hoping to cut from its wood a throne and a bed for herself. But as the tree grows, a snake [Ningishzida] makes its nest at its roots, Anzu settled in the top and in the trunk the demon makes her lair... Of greater importance, however, is the sexual aspect of the—mainly—female demons lilitu and lili. Thus the texts

---

[22] Special thanks to Doug Van Dorn for this "revelation." Van Dorn, Douglas (2013-01-21). *Giants: Sons of the Gods* (Kindle Locations 3922-3925). Waters of Creation. Kindle Edition. In fact, his "Chapter 13: Chimeras" was helpful for more than one insight in this appendix.

refer to them as the ones who have no husband, or as the ones who stroll about searching for men in order to ensnare them.[23]

Lilith was also known as the demon who stole away newborn babies to suck their blood, eat their bone marrow and consume their flesh.[24] In Jewish legends, she was described as having long hair and wings, and claimed to have been the first wife of Adam who was banished because of Adam's unwillingness to accept her as his equal.[25]

Lilith the "night hag" makes her appearance in the Bible in Isaiah 34 that we already saw included the mythical and demonic satyr. In this chapter, prophetic judgment upon Edom involves turning it into a desert wasteland that is inhabited by all kinds of demons; ravens, jackals, hyenas, satyrs — and Lilith.

> Isaiah 34:13-14 (RSV)
> It shall be the haunt of jackals... And wild beasts shall meet with hyenas, the satyr shall cry to his fellow; yea, there shall the night hag [*Lilith*] alight, and find for herself a resting place.

> Isaiah 34:14–15 (NASB95)
> [14] Yes, the night monster (*Lilith*) will settle there And will find herself a resting place. [15] The tree snake (*qippoz*) will make its nest and lay *eggs* there, And it will hatch and gather *them* under its protection.

Notice how the text talks about the owl that nests and lays and hatches her young in its shadow. Lexicons such as the *Theological Wordbook of the Old Testament* and *Brown, Driver, Briggs Hebrew Lexicon* contest this Hebrew word for owl (*qippoz*) with more ancient interpretations of an

---

[23] "Lilith," *DDD*, 520.

[24] Handy, Lowell K. "Lilith (Deity)". In *The Anchor Yale Bible Dictionary*, edited by David Noel Freedman. New York: Doubleday, 1992, 324-325.

[25] Ginzberg, Louis; Szold, Henrietta (2011-01-13). *Legends of the Jews*, all four volumes in a single file, improved 1/13/2011 (Kindle Locations 1016-1028). B&R Samizdat Express. Kindle Edition.

"arrow snake."[26] If they are correct, then the poetry of the passage would be more complete as the NASB indicates.

The snake of verse 15 would match the Lilith myth (v. 14) with the snake in the roots making its nest. The correlation is too close to deny that this is another Biblical reference to a popular mythic creature that the Bible writers refer to in demonic terms.

A Demon by Any Other Name...

So we find that God himself demonizes his opponents. He renames evil people and their ideas with demonic name-calling, he mocks pagan myths and uses their own images against them, and he reveals that the pagan gods are actually demonic principalities and powers that rule with heavenly authority behind earthly authorities. He calls it like it is.

Perhaps we should take a lesson from the Living God and begin to break through the euphemisms of our modern culture that cover over reality with obscuring language. Perhaps we should call out the evil by demonizing it as God does in his holy Word. Perhaps we should demonize the stigma of "demonizing" because in fact, there really are demons that need to be called out and addressed for what they really are: evil.

---

[26] 2050a, קִפּוֹז *Theological Wordbook of the Old Testament*, ed. R. Laird Harris, Gleason L. Archer, Jr. and Bruce K. Waltke, electronic ed., 806 (Chicago: Moody Press, 1999).
קִפּוֹז Brown, Francis, Samuel Rolles Driver, and Charles Augustus Briggs. *Enhanced Brown-Driver-Briggs Hebrew and English Lexicon*. electronic ed. Oak Harbor, WA: Logos Research Systems, 2000.

CHAPTER 2

Old Testament Storytelling Apologetics

This chapter has been adapted from the article, "Old Testament Storytelling Apologetics" in the Christian Research Journal Vol. 34 / No. 03 / 2011.

The pantheon of gods assembles to battle the chaos monster to protect their territory and kingdom. When the waters of the heavens part, the sea dragon of chaos breaks through and leaves destruction in its wake. The pantheon fights the sea dragon and its monster allies until it is stopped in its tracks by the mighty storm god.

Those who are educated in ancient Near Eastern mythopoeia will recognize this storyline as the Canaanite epic of Baal and Leviathan or the Babylonian epic of Marduk and Tiamat the sea dragon. But what they may not know is that it is also the storyline of the 2012 Marvel blockbuster movie, *The Avengers*. The purpose of bringing up this point is to call attention to the modern relevancy of this ancient narrative before we descend into the turbulent sea of ancient mythological memes and motifs that are too quickly written off as petty scholarly obsession with obscure archaic minutia that fail to connect to our lives in the modern world. Leviathan vs. the Storm God is a tale we are still retelling today in cultures both religious and secular.

For many Christians, the word *apologetics* conjures a picture of defending the faith with philosophical arguments, archeological evidence, historical inquiry, and other rational and empirical forms of discourse. Apologetics also involves *polemics*, which are aggressive arguments against the opposition. Sometimes a good offense is the best defense. But what is often missed in some apologetic strategies is the Biblical use of imagination. This is illustrative of a distinct imbalance when one considers that the Bible is only about one-third propositional truth and about two-thirds imagination: image, metaphor, poetry, and story.[1]

With the discovery in the nineteenth and twentieth centuries of pagan religious texts from ancient Near Eastern (ANE) cultures such as Babylon, Assyria, and Ugarit, Biblical scholarship has discovered many literary parallels between Scripture and the literature of ancient Israel's enemies. The Hebrews shared many words, images, concepts, metaphors, and narrative genres in common with their neighbors. And those Hebrew authors of Scripture sometimes incorporated similar literary imagination into their text.

With regard to these Biblical and ancient Near Eastern literary parallels, liberal scholarship tends to stress the similarities, downplay the differences, and construct a theory of the evolution of Israel's religion from polytheism to monotheism.[2] In other words, liberal scholarship is anthropocentric, or human-centered. Conservative scholarship tends to stress the differences, downplay the similarities, and interpret the evidence as indicative of the radical otherness of Israelite religion.[3] In other words, conservative scholarship is theocentric, or God-centered. In this way, both liberal and conservative hermeneutics err on opposite extremes.

The orthodox doctrine of the inspiration of Scripture states that it is composed of "God-breathed" human-written words (2 Tim. 3:16). Men wrote from God, moved by the Holy Spirit (2 Pet. 1:20–21). This is a "both/and" reality of humanly and heavenly authorship. While I affirm the heavenly side of God's Word, in this essay I will illustrate how the writers of the Old Testament both appropriated *and* subverted the story, imagery, and metaphor of their religious enemies as a polemic against those enemies' religion and deities. First, we will look at one of the princes of those pagan deities: Baal.

---

[1] I discuss this fact and its ramifications in my book *Word Pictures: Knowing God through Story and Imagination* (Downers Grove, IL: InterVarsity Press, 2009).

[2] A significant author of this view is Mark S. Smith, *The Origins of Biblical Monotheism: Israel's Polytheistic Background and the Ugaritic Texts* (Oxford: Oxford University, 2003).

[3] A significant author of this view is Gleason L. Archer, *A Survey of Old Testament Introduction* (Chicago: Moody Press, 2007).

Baal in Canaan

In 1929, an archeological excavation at a mound in northern Syria called Ras Shamra unearthed the remains of a significant port city called Ugarit, whose developed culture reaches back as far as 3000 B.C..[4] Among the important finds were literary tablets that opened the door to a deeper understanding of ancient Near Eastern culture and the Bible. Those tablets included Syro-Canaanite religious texts of pagan deities mentioned in the Old Testament. One of those deities was Baal.

Though the Semitic noun *baal* means "lord" or "master," it was also used as the proper name of the Canaanite storm god.[5] In the Baal narrative cycle from Ugarit, El was the supreme "father of the gods," who lived on a cosmic mountain. A divine council of gods called "Sons of El" surrounded him, vying for position and power. When Sea is coronated by El and given a palace, Baal rises up and kills Sea, taking Sea's place as "most high" over the other gods (excepting El). A temple is built and a feast celebrated. Mot (Death) then insults Baal, who goes down to the underworld, only to be defeated by Mot. But Anat, Baal's violent sister, seeks Mot and cuts him up into pieces and brings Baal's body back up to earth where he is brought back to life, only to fight Mot to a stalemate.[6]

The Dictionary of Deities and Demons in the Bible explains of Baal:

> "His elevated position shows itself in his power over clouds, storm and lightning, and manifests itself in his thundering voice. As the god of wind and weather Baal dispenses dew, rain, and snow and the attendant fertility of the soil. Baal's rule guarantees the annual return of the vegetation; as the god disappears in the underworld and returns in the autumn, so the vegetation dies and resuscitates with him."[7]

---

[4] Avraham Negev, "Ugarit," *The Archaeological Encyclopedia of the Holy Land*, 3rd ed. (New York: Prentice Hall Press, 1996).
[5] Karel van der Toorn, Bob Becking, and Pieter Willem van der Horst, *Dictionary of Deities and Demons in the Bible (DDD)*, 2nd ext. rev. ed. (Grand Rapids: Eerdmans, 1999), 132.
[6] N. Wyatt, *Religious Texts from Ugarit*, 2nd ed., The Biblical Seminar, vol. 53 (London: Sheffield Academic Press, 2002), 36–39.
[7] "Baal," *DDD*, 134.

Baal in the Bible

In the Bible, Baal is used both as the name of a specific deity[8] and as a generic term for multiple idols worshipped by apostate Israel.[9] It was also used in conjunction with city names and locations, such as Baal-Hermon and Baal-Zaphon, indicating manifestations of the one deity worshipped in a variety of different Canaanite situations.[10] Simply speaking, in Canaan, Baal was all over the place. He was the chief god of the land.

Upon entering Canaan, Yahweh gave specific instructions to the Israelites to destroy all the places where the Canaanites worshipped, along with their altars and images (Deut. 12:1–7). They were to "destroy the names" of the foreign idols and replace them with Yahweh's name and habitation (vv. 3–4). God warned them, "Take care lest your heart be deceived, and you turn aside and serve other gods and worship them" (Deut. 11:16).

Yet, turning to other gods in worship is exactly what the Israelites did — over and over again. No sooner had the people settled in Canaan than they began to adopt Baal worship into their culture. The book of Judges describes this cycle of idolatry under successive leaders (Judg. 2:11; 3:7; 8:33). In the ninth century B.C., Elijah fought against rampant Baal worship throughout Israel (1 Kgs. 18). In the eighth century, Hosea decried the adulterous intimacy that both Judah and Israel had with Baal (Hos. 2:13, 16–17), and in the seventh century, Jeremiah battled with an infestation of it in Judah (Jer. 2:23; 32:35).

Baal worship was so cancerous throughout Israel's history that Yahweh would have to intervene periodically with dramatic displays of authority in order to stem the infection that polluted the congregation of the Lord. Gideon's miraculous deliverances from the Baal-loving Midianites (Judg. 6–8) and Elijah's encounter with the prophets of Baal (1 Kgs. 18) are just a couple examples of Yahweh's real-world polemic against Baal. If Baal is god, "let him contend for himself, because his altar is broken down" (Judg. 6) and "the God who answers by fire, He is God!" (1 Kgs. 18:24). I call that

---

[8] Judg. 6; 1 Kgs. 18; 2 Kgs. 10.
[9] Judg. 2:13; 1 Sam. 12:10; Jer. 2:23.
[10] "Baal," *DDD*, 136.

"power polemics." But physical battles and miraculous signs and wonders are not the only way God waged war against Baal in ancient Canaan. He also used story, image, and metaphor. He used subversive literary imagination.

Yahweh Vs. Baal

Literary subversion was common in the ancient world to effect the overthrow or overshadowing of one deity and worldview with another. For example, the high goddess Inanna, considered Queen of Heaven in ancient Sumeria, was replaced by her Babylonian counterpart, Ishtar. An important Sumerian text, *The Descent of Inanna into the Underworld*, was rewritten by the Babylonians as *the Descent of Ishtar into the Underworld* to accommodate their goddess Ishtar.[11] The Babylonian creation epic, *Enuma Elish* tells the story of the Babylonian deity Marduk and his ascendancy to power in the Mesopotamian pantheon, giving mythical justification to the rise of Babylon as an ancient world power in the early eighteenth century B.C..[12] And then when King Sennacherib of Assyria conquered Babylon around 689 B.C., Assyrian scribes rewrote the *Enuma Elish* and replaced the name of Marduk with Assur, their chief god.[13]

Picture this scenario: The Israelites have left Egypt where Yahweh literally mocked and defeated the gods of Egypt through the ten plagues (Exod. 12:12; Num. 33:4). Pharaoh claimed to be a god, who according to Egyptian texts was the "possessor of a strong arm" and a "strong hand."[14] So when Yahweh repeatedly hammers home the message that Israel will be delivered by Yahweh's "strong arm" and "strong hand," the polemical irony is not hard to spot. Yahweh used subversive literary imagery, which in effect said, "Pharaoh is not God, I am God." Nothing like an arm wrestling match to show who is stronger. Later, in the time of Ezekiel, God would liken

---

[11] Stephanie Dalley, trans., *Myths from Mesopotamia: Creation, The Flood, Gilgamesh and Others* (New York: Oxford University Press, 1989, 2000, 2008), 154–62. The Sumerian version can be found in Jeremy Black, trans., *The Literature of Ancient Sumer* (New York: Oxford University Press **2004, 2006**), 65–76.

[12] Alexander Heidel, trans., *The Babylonian Genesis* (Chicago: University of Chicago, 1942, 1951, 1963), 14.

[13] C. Jouco Bleeker and Geo Widengren, eds., *Historia Religionum I: Religions of the Past* (Leiden, Netherlands: E. J. Brill, 1969), 134.

[14] John D. Currid, *Ancient Egypt and the Old Testament* (Grand Rapids: Baker; 1997), 83.

Pharaoh to a dragon in the Nile that He would draw out with a hook in his jaws (Ezek. 29:1-5) — polemical metaphors abounding.

But now, God is leading Israel into the Promised Land, which is very different from where they came, with very different gods. "For the land that you are entering to take possession of it is not like the land of Egypt, from which you have come, where you sowed your seed and irrigated it, like a garden of vegetables. But the land that you are going over to possess is a land of hills and valleys, which drinks water by the rain from heaven" (Deut. 11:10–11). And the god of rain from heaven in this new land was believed to be the storm god, Baal.[15] Yahweh therefore would relate to the Israelites in new and different terms related to a new and different world.

A look at some Ugaritic texts will give us a literary description of the Baal that Israel faced in Canaan. A side-by-side sampling of those Ugaritic texts with Scripture illustrates a strong reflection of Canaanite echoes in the Biblical storytelling.

UGARITIC TEXTS[16]	OLD TESTAMENT
Baal sits...	"Yahweh came from Sinai...
in the midst of his divine mountain, Saphon,	At His right hand there was flashing
in the midst of the mountain of victory.	lightning...
Seven lightning-flashes,	
eight bundles of thunder,	There is none like the God of Jeshurun,
a tree-of-lightning in his right hand.	Who rides the heavens to your help,
His head is magnificent,	And through the clouds in His majesty...
His brow is dew-drenched.	
his feet are eloquent in wrath.	And He drove out the enemy from before
(KTU 1.101:1–6)[17]	you,
	And said, 'Destroy!'
	So Israel dwells in security,
The season of his rains may Baal indeed	The fountain of Jacob secluded,
appoint,	In a land of grain and new wine;
the season of his storm-chariot.	

[15] Fred E. Woods, *Water and Storm Polemics against Baalism in the Deuteronomic History*, American University Studies, Series VII, Theology and Religion (New York: Peter Lange Publishing, 1994), 32–35.

[16] The abbreviation *KTU* stands for "Keilalphabetische Texte aus Ugarit", the standard collection of this material from Ugarit.

[17] All these Ugaritic texts can be found in N. Wyatt, *Religious Texts from Ugarit*, 2nd ed., The Biblical Seminar, vol. 53 (London: Sheffield Academic Press, 2002).

And the sound of his voice from the clouds, his hurling to the earth of lightning-flashes (KTU 1.4:5.5–9)	His heavens also drop down dew." (Deut. 33:2, 26–28)
At his holy voice the earth quaked; at the issue of his lips the mountains were afraid. The ancient mountains were afraid; the hills of the earth tottered. (KTU 1.4:7.30–35)	The voice of the LORD is over the waters; the God of glory thunders, the LORD, over many waters... The voice of the LORD breaks the cedars; the LORD breaks the cedars of Lebanon...
now your foe, Baal, now your foe the Sea you must smite; now you must destroy your adversary! Take your everlasting kingdom, your eternal dominion! (KTU 1.2:4.9–10)	The voice of the LORD flashes forth flames of fire [lightning]. The voice of the LORD shakes the wilderness...
Then Baal returned to his house [temple]. 'Will either king or commoner establish for himself dominion in the earth? (KTU 1.4:7.30–35)	And in His temple everything says, "Glory!" Yahweh sits enthroned over the flood; Yahweh is enthroned as King forever. (Psa. 29:3–11)

Like the usage of Yahweh's "strong arm" to poetically argue against the so-called "strong arm" of Pharaoh, so Yahweh inspires His authors to use water and storm language to reflect God's polemic against the so-called storm god Baal.

Comparing the texts yields identical words, memes, and metaphors that suggest God is engaging in polemics against Baal through scriptural imagery and storytelling. It is not Baal who rides his cloud chariot from his divine mountain Saphon, it is Yahweh who rides the clouds from His divine Mount Sinai (and later, Mount Zion). It is not Baal who hurls lightning flashes in wrath; it is Yahweh whose lightning flashes destroy His enemies. It is not Baal whose dew-drenched brow waters the land of Canaan; it is Yahweh who drops dew from heaven to Canaan. It is not Baal's voice that thunders and conquers the waters resulting in his everlasting temple enthronement, it is Yahweh whose voice thunders and conquers the waters resulting in His everlasting temple enthronement.

Psalm 29 (quoted in part above) is so replete with poetry in common with Canaanite poetry that many ANE scholars have concluded it is a Canaanite hymn to Baal that has been rewritten with the name Baal replaced by the name Yahweh.[18] God was not only *physically* dispossessing Canaan of its inhabitants, He was *literarily* dispossessing the Canaanite gods as well. Old Testament appropriation of Canaanite culture is a case of subversion, not syncretism — overthrowing cultural narratives as opposed to blending with them.

But this is only a glance at a single page of a book-load of resonances between Canaanite and Hebrew poetry. A closer look at comparing just two elements of the Baal cycle with Yahweh's story will yield a clearer picture of the literary subversion of the Canaanite narrative that God and the human authors were employing. Those two elements are the epithet of "cloud-rider" and God's conflict with the dragon and the sea.

Mount Zaphon/Sapon

Another element of Baal's reign that was just touched upon is his mountain abode of Mount Saphon (*Zaphon* in Hebrew). As written above, a plethora of Ugaritic texts link Baal with his "divine mountain, Saphon" (KTU 1.101:1-9; 1.100:9; 1.3:3:29), that he is buried there (KTU 1.6:1:15–18), his sanctuary (KTU 1.3:3:30), and mountain of victory (KTU 1.101:1–4). Earlier Hurrian and Hittite traditions of Baal link Mount Zaphon with another mountain, Namni, both in the northern Syrian ranges.[19]

This linking of the two mountains is of particular importance because as the *Dictionary of Deities and Demons* in the Bible explains, the Psalmist asserts Yahweh's authority as creator and therefore owner of all the heavens

---

[18] Aloysius Fitzgerald, "A Note on Psalm 29," *Bulletin of the American Schools of Oriental Research*, no. 215 (October 1974), 62. A more conservative interpretation claims a common Semitic poetic discourse.

[19] H. Niehr, "Zaphon", in *Dictionary of Deities and Demons in the Bible*, ed. Karel van der Toorn, Bob Becking and Pieter W. van der Horst, 2nd extensively rev. ed., 927 (Leiden; Boston; Köln; Grand Rapids, MI; Cambridge: Brill; Eerdmans, 1999).

and the earth by referring to the mountains of pagan mythology as under the lordship of Yahweh.

Psalm 89:12

The north (*zaphon*) and the south (*yamin*), you have created them; Tabor and Hermon joyously praise your name.

Tabor and Hermon are well known holy mountains within Canaanite and other mythology. But the deliberate linking of Zaphon and Yamin are most likely Hebrew references to the Saphon and Namni of Ugarit.

In Isaiah 14:13, Isaiah mocks the arrogance of the king of Babylon by likening him to another mythological figure, Athtar, who sought to take Baal's throne and failed "on the mountain of assembly on the summit of Zaphon."[20] In Psalm 48:1-2 Yahweh's holy mountain Zion replaces Mount Saphon as the divine mountain par excellence.[21]

Cloud-Rider

In the Ugaritic text cited above, we are introduced to Baal as one who rides the heavens in his cloud-chariot dispensing judgment from the heights. "Charioteer (or 'Rider') of the Clouds" was a common epithet ascribed to Baal throughout the Ugaritic texts.[22] Here is another side-by-side comparison of Ugaritic and Biblical texts that illustrate that common motif.

UGARITIC TEXTS	OLD TESTAMENT
'Dry him up. O Valiant Baal!	"[Yahweh] bowed the heavens also, and
Dry him up, O Charioteer [Rider] of the	came down

---

[20] Michael Heiser, "The Mythological Provenance of Isaiah 14:12-15: A Reconsideration of the Ugaritic Material" Liberty University <http://digitalcommons.liberty.edu/lts fac pubs/280>

[21] H. Niehr, "Zaphon", in *Dictionary of Deities and Demons in the Bible*, ed. Karel van der Toorn, Bob Becking and Pieter W. van der Horst, 2nd extensively rev. ed., 929 (Leiden; Boston; Köln; Grand Rapids, MI; Cambridge: Brill; Eerdmans, 1999). Also see Job 26:7; 37:22; Ezek. 1:4 where the word "north" is used as a spiritual reference, more allusion to the divine mountain Saphon of Canaanite belief.

[22] KTU 1.2:4.8-9; 1.3:3.38-41; 1.3:4:4, 6, 26; 1.4:3:10, 18; 1.4:5:7, 60; 1.10:1:7; 1.10:3:21, 36; 1.19:1:43; 1.92:37, 39.

Clouds!	With thick darkness under His feet.
For our captive is Prince Yam [Sea],	"And He rode on a cherub and flew;
for our captive is Ruler Nahar [River]!'	And He appeared on the wings of the wind.
(KTU 1.2:4.8–9)	"And He made darkness canopies around Him,
	A mass of waters, thick clouds of the sky.
What manner of enemy has arisen against Baal,	(2 Sam. 22:7–12)
of foe against the Charioteer of the Clouds?	
Surely I smote the Beloved of El, Yam [Sea]?	[Yahweh] makes the clouds His chariot;
Surely I exterminated Nahar [River], the mighty god?	He walks upon the wings of the wind;
Surely I lifted up the dragon,	(Psa. 104:3–4)
I overpowered him?	Behold, the LORD is riding on a swift cloud
I smote the writhing serpent,	and is about to come to Egypt;
Encircler-with-seven-heads!	The idols of Egypt will tremble at His presence,
(KTU 1.3:3.38–41)	(Isa. 19:1)

Yahweh is described here with the same exact moniker as Baal, in the same exact context as Baal — revealed in the storm and riding a cloud in judgment on other deities.

Baal the storm god is subverted by Yahweh, the God of storm.

The Dragon and the Sea

The second narrative element of the Canaanite Baal cycle that I want to address is God's conflict with the dragon and the sea. In ancient Near Eastern religious mythologies, the sea and the sea dragon were symbols of chaos that had to be overcome to bring order to the universe, or more exactly, the political world order of the myth's originating culture. Some scholars call this battle *Chaoskampf* — the divine struggle to create order out of chaos.[23] Creation accounts were often veiled polemics for the establishment of a king or kingdom's claim to sovereignty.[24] Richard Clifford quotes, "In Mesopotamia, Ugarit, and Israel the *Chaoskampf*

---

[23] Hermann Gunkel first suggested this theme in *Schöpfung und Chaos in Urzdt und Endzeit* (1895).

[24] Bruce R. Reichenbach, "Genesis 1 as a Theological-Political Narrative of Kingdom Establishment," *Bulletin for Biblical Research* 13, 1 (2003).

appears not only in cosmological contexts but just as frequently — and this was fundamentally true right from the first — in political contexts. The repulsion and the destruction of the enemy, and thereby the maintenance of political order, always constitute one of the major dimensions of the battle against chaos."[25]

For example, the Sumerians had three stories where the gods Enki, Ninurta, and Inanna all destroy sea monsters in their pursuit of establishing order. The sea monster in two of those versions, according to Sumerian expert Samuel Noah Kramer, is "conceived as a large serpent which lived in the bottom of the 'great below' where the latter came in contact with the primeval waters."[26] In the Babylonian creation myth, *Enuma Elish*, Marduk battles the sea dragon goddess Tiamat, and splits her body into two parts, creating the heavens and the earth, the world order over which Babylon's deity Marduk ruled.

Another side-by-side comparison of those same Ugaritic passages that we considered above with *other* Old Testament passages reveals another common narrative: Yahweh, the charioteer of the clouds, metaphorically battles with Sea (Hebrew: *yam*) and River (Hebrew: *nahar*), just as Baal struggled with Yam and Nahar, which is also linked to victory over a sea dragon/serpent.

UGARTIC TEXTS	OLD TESTAMENT
'Dry him up. O Valiant Baal!	Did Yahweh rage against the rivers,
Dry him up, O Charioteer of the Clouds!	Or was Your anger against the rivers (*nahar*),
For our captive is Prince Yam [Sea],	Or was Your wrath against the sea (*yam*),
for our captive is Ruler Nahar [River]!'	That You rode on Your horses,
(KTU 1.2:4.8–9)[27]	On Your chariots of salvation?
	(Hab. 3:8)
What manner of enemy has arisen against	
Baal,	In that day Yahweh will punish Leviathan
of foe against the Charioteer of the Clouds?	the fleeing serpent,

[25] Clifford, *Creation Accounts*, 8, n. 13.

[26] Samuel Noah Kramer, *Sumerian Mythology: A Study of Spiritual and Literary Achievement in the Third Millennium B.C.* (Philadelphia: University of Pennsylvania Press, 1944, 1961, 1972), 77–78.

[27] "Charioteer of the Clouds" also appears in these texts: KTU 1.3:4:4, 6, 26; 1.4:3:10, 18; 1.4:5:7, 60; 1.10:1:7; 1.10:3:21, 36; 1.19:1:43; 1.92:37, 39.

Surely I smote the Beloved of El, Yam [Sea]? Surely I exterminated Nahar [River], the mighty god? Surely I lifted up the dragon, I overpowered him? I smote the writhing serpent, Encircler-with-seven-heads! (KTU 1.3:3.38–41)	With His fierce and great and mighty sword, Even Leviathan the twisted serpent; And He will kill the dragon who lives in the sea. (Isa. 27:1) "You divided the sea by your might; you broke the heads of the sea monsters on the waters. You crushed the heads of Leviathan. (Psa. 74:13–14)

Baal fights Sea and River to establish his sovereignty. He wins by drinking up Sea and River, draining them dry, and thus establishing his supremacy over the pantheon and the Canaanite world order.[28] In the second passage, Baal's battle with Sea and River is retold in other words as a battle with a "dragon," the "writhing serpent" with seven heads.[29] Another Baal text calls this same dragon, "*Lotan, the wriggling serpent.*"[30] The Hebrew equivalents of the Ugaritic words *tannin* (dragon) and *lotan* are *tanniyn* (dragon) and *liwyatan* (Leviathan) respectively.[31] Thus, the Canaanite narrative of Leviathan the sea dragon or serpent is undeniably employed in Old Testament Scriptures.[32] Notice the last Scripture in the chart that refers to Leviathan as having multiple heads *just like the Canaanite Leviathan.*

And notice as well the reference to the Red Sea event also associated with Leviathan in the Biblical text. In Psalm 74 above, God's parting of the waters is connected to the motif of the Mosaic covenant as the creation of a new world order in the same way that Baal's victory over the waters and the dragon are emblematic of his establishment of authority in the Canaanite pantheon. This covenant motif is described as a *chaoskampf* battle with the

---

[28] KTU 1.2:4:27–32.
[29] See KTU 1.5:1:1–35.
[30] KTU 1.5:1:1–4.
[31] Walter C. Kaiser, Jr., *The Ugaritic Pantheon* (dissertation) (Ann Arbor, MI: Brandeis University, 1973), 212.
[32] See also Is. 51:9; Ezek. 32:2; Rev. 12:9, 16, 17.

Sea and Leviathan (called *Rahab*) in several other significant Biblical references as well.[33]

Subverting Paganism

When it comes to comparative studies between the Bible and other ANE mythopoeia, confessing scholarship tends to operate under a faith commitment to overwrought supernaturalism. It paints a picture of Israel's mythopoeia as wholly other or completely alien to its surroundings, as if this is what is needed to secure religious authority behind the text. The evidence clearly contradicts such theories of "divine dictation" or modern notions of science and history. The humanity of Scriptural authorship does not negate providential divine authorship. But critical scholarship tends to operate under a faith commitment to anti-supernaturalism. Therefore it interprets common story motifs between Baal and Yahweh as evidence of evolutionary transformation of one religion into another — of polytheism into monotheism. They reduce the Bible to derivative "mythology" that plagiarizes or borrows from its pagan neighbors. The discerning reader need not fall for the cultural imperialism of either of these modernist narratives.

Common imagination springs from what John Walton calls a "common cognitive environment" of people in a shared space, time, or culture. Walton suggests, "Borrowing is not the issue [...] Likewise this need not concern whose ideas are derivative. There is simply common ground across the cognitive environment of the cultures of the ancient world."[34] The story of a Cloud-rider controlling the elements and battling the Sea and Leviathan to establish his sovereignty over other gods with a new world order is not a false "myth," it is a narrative shared between Israel and her pagan neighbors that Jewish authors appropriate, with divine approval of Yahweh, as a metaphor within their own discourse. And that discourse involves subversion, the replacement or overthrow of the opponent's worldview with one's own.

---

[33] Ps. 89:9–10; Isa. 51:9–10; Job 26:12–13. Psa. 18, 29, 24, 29, 65, 74, 77, 89, 93, and 104 all reflect *chaoskampf*. See also Exod. 15, Job 9, 26, 38, and Isa. 51:14-16; 2 Sam. 22.

[34] John H. Walton, *Ancient Near Eastern Thought and the Old Testament: Introducing the Conceptual World of the Hebrew Bible* (Grand Rapids: Baker, 2006), 21.

It is no different than what we do today, as we moderns use the current science narratives of string theory or multiverses to construct our worldview and spin our science fiction just as ancient man did with the Mesopotamian or Ptolemaic universe. And as writers well know, science fiction is a morality tale about where our current cultural values will lead us in the future. Or we see the narrative of atheistic evolution seek to reduce morality, altruism, and religion into categories of its own construction and control. Political opponents on all sides in the Media construct narratives to control public discourse. The real revelation is that subversion of narrative is not a special technique used only by activists and intellectuals. It is the very nature of most storytelling through history. We are all creatures of our times seeking to control the narrative of our times, just as the ancients did. And those who control the cultural narrative, control the culture.

Great fathers of the Christian Faith subverted their cultural narrative. Curtis Chang, in his book, *Engaging Unbelief*, examines the apologetic work of church fathers Augustine and Aquinas. Augustine lived within the Roman Empire whose cultural narrative was the history of the "Eternal City." So the Bishop of Hippo wrote his *City of God* to defend the Christian faith in terms of urban historical narrative saturated with references, motifs, and themes from classical Roman authors like Virgil and Marcus Varro. He subverted that "City of Man" by revealing the destructive pride lurking behind all human social construction. Aquinas, in his *Summa contra Gentiles*, appealed to the Aristotelian story of knowledge because he was addressing a Muslim culture steeped in Aristotle. But he subverted that cultural narrative by teasing out the ultimate insufficiency of human reason. Augustine and Aquinas changed their worlds through subversive literary metaphor.

Chang explains this rhetorical strategy as threefold: "1. Entering the challenger's story, 2. Retelling the story, 3. Capturing that retold tale with the gospel metanarrative." He writes that the challenge of each epoch in history is a contest in storytelling, a challenge to "overturn and supplant the inherited story of the epoch with its own metanarrative [...] The one who can tell the best story, in a very real sense, wins the epoch." [35]

---

[35] Ibid., 27.

The hostile "post-Christian" epoch in which we live requires enterprising believers to retell the narratives of our culture with bold fresh perspectives. Tolkien and Lewis are among the finest modern examples of subversive authors who entered into the genres and mythology of pagan worlds to harness them for Christian imagination. Tolkien's Middle Earth abounded with the mythical Norse characters of wizards, dwarves, elves, giants, and trolls all in the service of his Catholic worldview. Lewis's Narnia is saturated with a plethora of beasts from assorted pagan mythologies, deliberately subjugated to the Lordship of Aslan. As a professional filmmaker I would add to these examples Mel Gibson's *Apocalypto,* that subversively enters the narrative of indigenous pagan earth religion in order to reveal it as barbarism based on human sacrifice. Scott Derrickson's *The Exorcism of Emily Rose* subverts the materialist narrative by depicting the supernatural on trial. Horror is a genre in all the arts that tends to be considered pagan or destructive. Yet horror is another genre that the "Holy Book" uses to subvert the evil its authors fight against. Who can deny the power of epic horror fantasy in the books of Daniel and Revelation that seek to turn the fear of man into the fear of God?

The problem is that some of those who revere the Bible as their sacred text fear that engaging pagan thought forms or motifs will corrupt their narrative, dilute the truth, and drag the believer into apostasy. Hopefully, this exploration of how the Biblical authors subverted pagan narratives of the Storm God versus Leviathan the Sea Dragon will provide a boost of confidence that will help free the believing storyteller and reader from the religious shackles of fear of the imagination. For as the great artistic intellect Francis Schaeffer once wrote, "The Christian is the really free man — he is free to have imagination. The Christian is the one whose imagination should fly beyond the stars."[36]

I am a filmmaker, so I think in terms of movies. We need more storytellers to tell vampire stories with a Christian worldview (*The Addiction*); more zombie stories with a Christian worldview (*I Am Legend*); more demonic stories with Christian redemption (M. Night Shyamalan's *Devil*); more post-apocalyptic thrillers that honor God (*The Book of Eli*);

---

[36] Schaeffer, Francis. *Art and the Bible.* Downers Grove: InterVarsity Press, 1973, 91.

more subversion of adultery (*Fatal Attraction*), fornication (*17 Again*), unbelief (*Paranormal Activity*), paganism (*Apocalypto*), humanistic anti-supernaturalism (*The Last Exorcism*), and our "pro-Choice" culture of death (*The Island*).

I will end with a question and a charge. With two exceptions, why were all these movies that subversively incarnate the Christian worldview made by non-Christians instead of Christians? Rise up, O Christian apologists and subvert ye the world's imagination!

CHAPTER 3

Biblical Creation and Storytelling

This chapter has been adapted from the article "Biblical Creation and Storytelling: Cosmos, Combat, and Covenant" published at BioLogos Foundation.

I am a professional storyteller. My interests lie in understanding the literary genres and cultural contexts of the Bible as it existed within an ancient Near Eastern worldview that included common metaphors, images, and concepts. As readers displaced from such an ancient world by time, space, and culture, we will misread the text through our own cultural prejudice if we do not seek to understand it through the eyes of its original writers and readers. Creation stories (cosmogonies) such as Genesis 1 are particularly vulnerable to this kind of interpretive violence.

Genesis 1 is an ancient cosmogony, a story of the origin of the universe. Its Semitic authorship is birthed within a varied cultural heritage of Babylonian, Egyptian and Canaanite environments. The orthodox Christian tradition claims that we have received the entire corpus of the Old Testament as "breathed out" by God through the writings and personalities of those human beings embedded within their cultures (2 Tim. 3:16; 1 Pet. 1:20-21). This doctrine of "dual authorship" between divinity and humanity is not a dictation theory or automatic writing, but rather a providential means of transmission of truth through incarnation of human literary convention.[1]

As an orthodox Christian, I affirm both the human and divine origin of the Bible with equal ultimacy. The differences between it and other ANE literature surely illustrate a divine antithesis, but the similarities between it and other ANE literature surely illustrate human synthesis that need not support the claim of untruth. God accommodates and uses human culture and

---

[1] "The Chicago Statement on Biblical Inerrancy," Article VIII, 1978: "We affirm that God in His Work of inspiration utilized the distinctive personalities and literary styles of the writers whom He had chosen and prepared. We deny that God, in causing these writers to use the very words that He chose, overrode their personalities."

conceptions to communicate His truth because we cannot comprehend God's kingdom outside of our finite paradigms of understanding. As John Calvin so aptly put it, "[I]t shows an extraordinary degree of wickedness, that we yield less reverence to God speaking to us, because He condescends to our ignorance; and, therefore, when God prattles to us in Scripture in a rough and popular style, let us know that this is done on account of the love which He bears to us."[2]

In light of this "loving accommodation" that Calvin spoke of, The Chicago Statement on Biblical Inerrancy (1978) concluded, "Differences between literary conventions in Bible times and in ours must also be observed… Scripture is inerrant, not in the sense of being absolutely precise by modern standards, but in the sense of making good its claims and achieving that measure of focused truth at which its authors aimed."[3]

So, what is "the measure of focused truth" at which the Biblical authors aimed? If it was not absolute precision by modern standards, as these conservative scholars admit, then what kind of truth was it? Let's take a look at some of the ANE literary and storytelling features of Scripture to see just what kind of truth God's word intended when it comes to Biblical creation.

Creation as Cosmogony

The 18th century "Age of Enlightenment" established autonomous human reasoning as the primary source of authority and elevated "scientific" empirical observation over abstract philosophy and theology. One of the effects of this cultural revolution on the way we think today is a materialist prejudice, the belief that ultimate reality is material, not spiritual. Any appeal to teleology or purpose behind natural events became illegitimate because the dominant assumption was that we live in a closed system of natural causes. So when we as moderns approach cosmogony, or the story of the origin of the universe, we naturally assume any such story is about answering the question of where matter comes from (since this is ultimate

---

[2] John Calvin, *Commentary on the Gospel According to John*, 3:12.
[3] The Chicago Statement on Biblical Inerrancy (1978), Exposition: "Infallibility, Inerrancy, Interpretation."

reality to us). Our post-Enlightened scientific minds demand "objective" descriptions of material structure, natural laws that work upon matter, and taxonomic categories of material substances.

But this is not the way the ancient Near Eastern mind thought when approaching cosmogony. To interpret ancient pre-scientific cosmogonies through our post-Enlightened scientific materialist categories is to do violence to the text, an act of cultural imperialism. As John Walton argues, "People in the ancient world believed that something existed not by virtue of its material properties, but by virtue of its having a function in an ordered system."[4] And that ordered system was not a scientific system of matter and physics, but a human system of society and culture.

Walton explains that creation and existence in the ANE mindset involved three elements alien to modern notions of existence. He lays out examples from Mesopotamian and Egyptian creation myths in common with Genesis to illustrate that bringing something into existence was not about "making things" or manufacturing material substance but about *naming, separating, and assigning roles to things.*[5]

Naming

Consider these ANE creation activities of naming:

• The Egyptian Memphite Theology describes Ptah creating everything by pronouncing its name.[6]

• The Babylonian Enuma Elish begins with the heavens and earth as well as the deities "not yet named," whose existence comes from being so named.[7]

---

[4] John H. Walton, *The Lost World of Genesis One: Ancient Cosmology and the Origins Debate* (Downers Grove: IL, InterVarsity Press, 2009), 26.
[5] John H. Walton, *Ancient Near Eastern Thought and the Old Testament: Introducing the Conceptual World of the Hebrew Bible* (Grand Rapids, MI: Baker, 2006) 188-189.
[6] James B. Pritchard, ed., *Ancient Near Eastern Texts Relating to the Old Testament* (Princeton, NJ: Princeton University, 1950, 1955), 5.
[7] Alexander Heidel, trans., *The Babylonian Genesis* (Chicago, IL: University of Chicago, 1942, 1951, 1963), 18.

- The Hebrew Genesis shows Yahweh naming things and calling them "good," a word not of moral quality, but of orderly fittingness.[8]

This is not so much a denial of *creatio ex nihilo*, (creation out of nothing) as it is a cultural linguistic focus on purposes over properties. "Thus, the [Hebrew] text never uses *bara* [a special word used exclusively of divine activity] in a context in which materials are mentioned...that materials are not mentioned suggests that manufacture is not the issue."[9]

Separation

Consider these ANE creation activities of separation:

- Everything in the Egyptian universe came into existence through separation from something else. The limitless ocean above the sky (the god Nun) was separated from the waters under the earth (Tefnut) by Shu, the god of air.[10]

- In the Babylonian Enuma Elish, the victorious Marduk created the heavens and the earth by splitting the corpse of his vanquished foe Tiamat in two.[11]

- In Genesis, God separated the light from the darkness (1:4), the waters above from the waters below (1:6-7), the land from the waters below (1:9), male from female (2:21-24), and the Sabbath from other days (2:3).

Separation is differentiation or distinction between things. God separates a people for Himself (1 Sam. 12:22), and gives great detail in the Law from Sinai for cultic separations that reinforce a code of holiness. The

---

[8] Walton, *The Lost World*, 51.
[9] Walton, Ancient Near Eastern Thought, 183.
[10] Pritchard, Ancient Near Eastern Thought, 6.
[11] Heidel, Babylonian Genesis, 42.

separation of creation is a theological reinforcement of God's majority theme of holy otherness in Scripture.

Roles

Consider these ANE creation activities of assigning roles:

- The Egyptian Papyrus Insinger describes 18 creations of functions for things from the earth to wealth.[12]

- The Babylonian Enuma Elish has Marduk creating sun, moon and constellations for their purposes, and specified stations for the gods.[13]

- Yahweh is described as creating the things-in-the-world of Genesis 1 by explaining their purposes: Light and dark to mark time (1:5); sun, moon, and stars to give light (1:16); and signs for seasons (1:14); plants and fruit for food (1:29); mankind to rule over animals and the creation (1:27-28).

Things-in-the-world were thought of in terms of their purpose for humankind not their material being. This stress on teleology (purpose) sheds light on the personification of nature into deities whose ANE stories become mythic explanations of cycles that are used instrumentally in religious cult.[14] Purpose can only come from persons, so pagan deities were immanent within nature. Though Yahweh was contrastingly transcendent He was nevertheless the person behind the purpose of the depersonalized nature. Thus, even

---

[12] Walton, *The Lost World*, 32-33.

[13] Heidel, *Babylonian Genesis*, 44-45.

[14] The Baal cycle tells the story of Baal, god of the storm, winds, and rain, being killed by Mot, the god of death. Baal's sister Anat, then defeats Mot and Baal is revived and the drought ends with the coming of rain. Michael David Coogan, trans. *Stories from Ancient Canaan* (Louisville, KY: Westminster Press), 84-85. In Egypt, a similar cycle of death and regeneration based on agriculture is found in such myths as Osiris. The "great god" Osiris is killed by his brother Seth, and "resurrected" as king by decree of the gods at the behest of Osiris's sister, Isis. Egyptians would worship Osiris as the god of agricultural fertility. Robert A. Armour, *Gods and Myths of Ancient Egypt* (Cairo, Egypt: American University in Cairo), 178-179.

Yahweh uses natural elements such as wind, lightning and thunderstorms as means of revealing His presence (theophany) and purposes.[15]

Interpreting the creation story of Genesis with an expectation of modern scientific discourse is hermeneutical violence. The notion of creation and existence in the Biblical ancient Near East was not one of physics, life sciences, material substance and structure, it was a story explaining the creation of the functions of the world through naming, separation and purpose. Purpose (teleology) is theological not empirical and does not therefore require any scientific theory, be it young earth creationism or theistic evolution.

Creation as Combat

In his analysis of ancient creation accounts, Richard Clifford concludes that "many ancient cosmogonies are narratives and depend on plot and character for their movement; they must be read as drama rather than 'objective' description."[16] To the ancients, creation was not a historical chronology of material origins, but a drama of spiritual purposes. The essence of drama is conflict, and that conflict is reflected in Biblical creation, no less than in ANE accounts, through the text as theological-political polemic — images of combat.

One of the functions of ancient creation narratives is to literarily encode the religious and political overthrow of one culture by another. When a king or kingdom would rise to power in the ancient world, they would often displace the vassal culture's creation stories with their own stories of how their deities triumphed over others to create the world in which they now lived.

The Enuma Elish tells the story of the Babylonian deity Marduk, and his ascendancy to power in the Mesopotamian pantheon, giving mythical justification to the rise of Babylon as an ancient world power most likely in

---

[15] Ronald A. Simkins, *Creator and Creation: Nature in the Worldview of Ancient Israel* (Peabody, MA: Hendrickson, 1994, 2003) 145-146.
[16] Richard J. Clifford, *Creation Accounts in the Ancient Near East and in the Bible*, Catholic Biblical Quarterly Monograph Series 26 (Washington D.C.: Catholic Biblical Association of America, 1994), 199.

the First Babylonian Dynasty under Hammurabi (1792-1750 B.C.).[17] As the prologue of the Code of Hammurabi explains, "Anu, the majestic, King of the Anunnaki, and Bel, the Lord of Heaven and Earth, who established the fate of the land, had given to Marduk, the ruling son of Ea, dominion over mankind, and called Babylon by his great name; when they made it great upon the earth by founding therein an eternal kingdom, whose foundations are as firmly grounded as are those of heaven and earth."[18]

The Baal myth of Ugarit tells the story of the storm god "Baal the Conqueror," and his epiphany in becoming "Lord of the earth" in Canaan.[19] Chapter I of the text reads,

> "Let me tell you, Prince Baal,
>
> let me repeat, Rider on the Clouds:
>
> Behold, your enemy, Baal,
>
> behold, you will kill your enemy,
>
> behold, you will annihilate your foes.
>
> You will take your eternal kingship,
>
> your dominion forever and ever."[20]

Genesis 1, according to scholar Bruce Reichenbach, was also written "as a theological-political document that describes how the Supreme Monarch establishes His kingdom and thereby justifies His claim to exclusive possession of everything in it."[21] If Moses wrote Genesis, it would make sense that he would appropriate the creation story genre as he learned it from the Egyptians. Respected Egyptian translator John Wilson wrote regarding the Egyptian creation genre. "Every important cult-center of Egypt asserted its primacy by the dogma that it was the site of creation."[22]

---

[17] Heidel, *Babylonian Genesis*, 14.

[18] W.W. Davies, *The Codes of Hammurabi and Moses: With Copious Comments, Index, and Bible References* (Berkeley, CA: Apocryphile Press, 1905, 2006), 17.

[19] Coogan, *Stories from Ancient Canaan*, 75-115.

[20] Coogan, *Stories from Ancient Canaan*, 88.

[21] Bruce R. Reichenbach, "Genesis 1 as a Theological-Political Narrative of Kingdom Establishment," *Bulletin for Biblical Research* 13.1 (2003), p. 48.

[22] *The Ancient Near East an Anthology of Texts and Pictures.*, ed. James Bennett Pritchard, 8 (Princeton: Princeton University Press, 1958).

God was preparing Israel to displace the pagan Canaanites and their gods both physically and literarily, so He inspired this authorship of the creation account to express that ancient Near Eastern motif of justifying transcendent authority and land ownership with a creation story that argued their God created the Edenic garden ("Promised Land") upon which they laid claim.[23]

Genesis follows the literary structure of suzerain-vassal treaties that reflects the activity of ancient Near Eastern monarchs. "God says and it happens, names and it is His, sets His representative images throughout the land, sits and pronounces in council, establishes the cultic, and is the ultimate arbiter of what is good."[24] It is distinctly polemical for the Genesis account to describe the common male and female as God's representatives, created in His image, since this concept seems only to be applied to kings in ancient Mesopotamia.[25]

Genesis 1 is the poetic legitimation of Yahweh, the God of Israel, and His authority and power over all things, including the gods of Canaan, who are in fact, reduced to nothing. The literary act of replacing one identity with another by investing new meaning into commonly understood words, images, metaphors or motifs is called "subversion."

This subversion of pagan deities in the text is also achieved through the demythologizing of nature. Mesopotamian, Canaanite and Egyptian cosmogonies all personify nature through their various deities of sun, moon, stars, waters and the heavens. These gods are mere personifications of nature and are therefore subject to the cycles and seasons of nature.

Contrarily, in Genesis 1 we see a specific description of Yahweh as sovereign creator and sustainer of seasons and their signs for His purposes. Nature has no animistic personality. When describing the creation of sun and moon, the Hebrew text seems to avoid the names for sun (*shemesh*) and moon (*chodesh*), perhaps because these words were also the names of ancient Near Eastern gods. Instead, the writer simply calls them the "greater" and "lesser" lights, heavenly bodies.

---

[23] Exod. 3:8; Num. 13:23-27.
[24] Reichenbach, "Genesis 1," 49.
[25] Edward Mason Curtis, *Man As The Image Of God In Genesis In The Light Of Ancient Near Eastern Parallels*, Dissertation (Philadelphia, PA: University of Pennsylvania).

When describing the surface of the deep over which the spirit of God hovered (Gen. 1:2), the author uses a word for the deep (*tehom*) with possible linguistic connections to ANE myths of a sea dragon, a symbol of the chaos out of which deity brings order.[26] While the Genesis account reflects a similar creation out of watery chaos, it nevertheless strips all animation from that watery chaos. It remains an inert lifeless state without personality, moldable in the hands of the Creator. Genesis subverts the ancient Near Eastern creation genre of literature by using common ANE narrative concepts and reinvesting them with new definitions and contexts.

Another way that Biblical creation reflects ancient Near Eastern culture, while subverting it is in its appropriation of what ANE scholars call the *Chaoskampf* motif, or the creation of order out of chaos through struggle. Hermann Gunkel first suggested in *Creation and Chaos* (1895) that some ancient Near Eastern creation myths contained a cosmic conflict between deity and sea, as well as sea dragons or serpents that expressed the creation of order out of chaos.[27] Gunkel argued that Genesis borrowed this idea from the Babylonian tale of Marduk battling the goddess Tiamat, serpent of chaos, whom he vanquished, and out of whose body he created the heavens and earth.[28] Later, John Day argued in light of the discovery of the Ugarit tablets in 1928, that Canaan, not Babylonia is the source of the combat motif in Genesis,[29] reflected in Yahweh's own complaint that Israel had become polluted by Canaanite culture.[30] In the Baal cycle, Baal battles Yam (Sea)

---

[26] John Day, *God's Conflict with the Dragon and the Sea: Echoes of a Canaanite myth in the Old Testament* (Great Britain: Cambridge University Press, 1985), 5.

[27] Hermann Gunkel, Heinrich Zimmern; K. William Whitney Jr., trans., *Creation And Chaos in the Primeval Era And the Eschaton: A Religio-historical Study of Genesis 1 and Revelation 12* (Grand Rapids: MI: Eerdmans, 1895, 1921, 2006), xvi.

[28] "He cast down her carcass and stood upon it.
After he had slain Tiamat, the leader…
He split her open like a mussel into two parts;
Half of her he set in place and formed the sky…
And a great structure, its counterpart, he established, namely Esharra [earth]."
(Enuma Elish, Tablet IV, lines 104-105, 137-138, 144 from Heidel, *Babylonian Genesis*, 41-42)

[29] John Day, *God's Conflict with the Dragon*. Day argues that the Canaanite Baal cycle implies a connection with creation, since it is a ritual fertility festival (cyclical creation) falling on the New Year, traditionally understood as the date of creation. But his strongest appeal is the argument in reverse that the Canaanite myth makes a connection between creation and *Chaoskampf* because the Old Testament does so.

[30] "Then the word of the LORD came to me, saying, "Son of man, make known to Jerusalem her abominations and say, 'Thus says the Lord GOD to Jerusalem, "Your origin and your

and conquers it, along with "the dragon," "the twisting serpent," to be enthroned as chief deity of the Canaanite pantheon.[31]

While the image of struggle has already been noted as being polemically absent in Genesis 1, it is certainly alive and kicking in other creation passages throughout the Old Testament. Rather than speculating about who borrowed whose understanding of *Chaoskampf,* Walton suggests "borrowing is not the issue... Likewise this need not concern whose ideas are derivative. There is simply common ground across the cognitive environment of the cultures of the ancient world."[32] *Chaoskampf* is simply a common ancient Near Eastern motif shared between Israel and its pagan neighbors that Jewish authors appropriate, under divine authority of Yahweh, for their own discourse. For Biblical authors, creation and *Chaoskampf* language are intertwined to describe the action of Yahweh creating His world order out of chaos — alternately symbolized as Sea, Leviathan, Dragon and Rahab.

> You broke the heads of the sea monsters in the waters.
> You crushed the heads of Leviathan;...
> You have prepared the light and the sun.
> You have established all the boundaries of the earth;
> (Psa. 74:12-17)

---

birth are from the land of the Canaanite, your father was an Amorite and your mother a Hittite." (Ezek. 16:1-3)

[31] "Didn't I [Baal] demolish El's Darling, Sea?
didn't I finish off the divine river, Rabbim?
didn't I snare the Dragon?
I enveloped him,
I demolished the Twisting Serpent,
the seven-headed monster.
(Baal II from Coogan, *Stories from Ancient Canaan,* 92.)
"When you [Baal] killed Lotan, the Fleeing Serpent,
finished off the Twisting Serpent,
the seven-headed monster,
the heavens withered and drooped."
(Baal IV from Coogan, *Stories from Ancient Canaan,* 106.)
Most recently, David Tsumura has argued against any connection of such mythic struggle in the Biblical text in favor of mere poetic flair: David Toshio Tsumura, *Creation And Destruction: A Reappraisal of the Chaoskampf Theory in the Old Testament* (Winona Lake, IN: Eisenbrauns, 2006).

[32] Walton, *Ancient Near Eastern Thought,* 21.

Was it not You who cut Rahab in pieces,
Who pierced the dragon?
Was it not You who dried up the sea,
The waters of the great deep;
[Y]ou have forgotten the LORD your Maker,
Who stretched out the heavens
And laid the foundations of the earth...
"For I am the LORD your God, who stirs up the sea and its
waves roar (the LORD of hosts is His name).
(Isa. 51:9-14)

You rule the swelling of the sea;
When its waves rise, You still them.
You Yourself crushed Rahab like one who is slain;
You scattered Your enemies with Your mighty arm.
The heavens are Yours, the earth also is Yours;
The world and all it contains, You have founded them.
The north and the south, You have created them;
(Psa. 89:6-12)

In that day the LORD will punish Leviathan the fleeing
serpent,
With His fierce and great and mighty sword,
Even Leviathan the twisted serpent;
And He will kill the dragon who lives in the sea.
(Isa. 27:1)

So the language of *Chaoskampf* in battling the sea/dragon/Leviathan/Rahab is an image that Israel had in common with its ancient Near Eastern pagan neighbors to describe God's creation of the cosmos.[33] The controversial difference lies in God's transcendent control *over* creation versus Canaanite or Mesopotamian immanent struggle *within* creation. God doesn't battle with the beasts like Baal or Marduk does, he

---

[33] See also Isa. 27:1; Psa. 77:16-18; Job 26:7-13.

sovereignly controls them and destroys them for his own purposes. Creation of cosmos out of chaos is not a great effort for the one God Yahweh of the Hebrew Scriptures.

But exactly what kind of cosmos does Yahweh create in the Biblical text? It is not the cosmos of material substance and physics, but rather the cosmos of God's covenant.

Creation as Covenant

Chaoskampf and creation language are used as word pictures for God's covenant activity in the Bible. For God, describing the creation of the heavens and earth was a way of saying He has established His covenant with His people through exodus into the Promised Land,[34] reaffirming that covenant with the kingly line of David, and finalizing the covenant by bringing them out of exile. The reader should understand that the Scriptures listed above, exemplary of *Chaoskampf,* were deliberately abbreviated to make a further point in this section. I will now add the missing text in those passages in bold to reveal a deeper motif at play in the text — a motif not of creation as mere material manufacturing, but of creation as covenantal formation. God redeeming His people and establishing His covenant with them is poetically likened to the suppression of the dragon of chaos and the creation of the cosmos.

> Yet God is my king from of old,
> Who works deeds of deliverance in the midst of the earth.
> You divided the sea by Your strength;
> **[A reference to the Exodus deliverance of the covenant at Sinai]**
> You broke the heads of the sea monsters in the waters.
> You crushed the heads of Leviathan;...
> You have prepared the light and the sun.
> You have established all the boundaries of the earth;
> (Psa. 74:12-17)

---

[34] John Owen, *Works*, 16 vols. (London: The Banner of Truth Trust, 1965-1968), Vol. 9 134.

Was it not You who cut Rahab in pieces,
Who pierced the dragon?
Was it not You who dried up the sea,
The waters of the great deep;
Who made the depths of the sea a pathway
For the redeemed to cross over?...
[Y]ou have forgotten the LORD your Maker,
Who stretched out the heavens
And laid the foundations of the earth...
"For I am the LORD your God, who stirs up the sea and its
waves roar (the LORD of hosts is His name). "I have put My
words in your mouth and have covered you with the shadow
of My hand, to establish the heavens, to found the earth, and
to say to Zion, 'You are My people.'"
[a reaffirmation of the Sinai covenant through Moses]
(Isa. 51:9-16)

You rule the swelling of the sea;
When its waves rise, You still them.
You Yourself crushed Rahab like one who is slain;
You scattered Your enemies with Your mighty arm.
The heavens are Yours, the earth also is Yours;
The world and all it contains, You have founded them.
The north and the south, You have created them...
"I have found David My servant;
With My holy oil I have anointed him,
With whom My hand will be established;
And in My name his horn will be exalted.
"I shall also set his hand on the sea
And his right hand on the rivers...
"My lovingkindness I will keep for him forever,
And My covenant shall be confirmed to him.
"So I will establish his descendants forever
And his throne as the days of heaven.

(Psa. 89:6-12,19-29)

In that day the LORD will punish Leviathan the fleeing
serpent,
With His fierce and great and mighty sword,
Even Leviathan the twisted serpent;
And He will kill the dragon who lives in the sea...
In the days to come Jacob will take root,
Israel will blossom and sprout,
And they will fill the whole world with fruit.
It will come about also in that day that a great trumpet will
be blown, and those who were perishing in the land of
Assyria and who were scattered in the land of Egypt will
come and worship the LORD in the holy mountain at
Jerusalem.
[the future consummation of the Mosaic and Davidic
covenant in the New Covenant of Messiah]
(Isa. 27:1, 6-13)

In these texts, and others,[35] God does not merely appeal to His power of
material creation as justification for the authority of His covenant, but more
importantly He uses the creation of the heavens and earth, involving
subjugation of the sea and dragon, as poetic descriptions of God's covenant
with His people, rooted in the Exodus story. The creation of the covenant is
the creation of the heavens and the earth. The covenant is a cosmos — not a
material one centered in astronomical location and abstract impersonal
forces as modern worldview demands, but a theological one, centered in the
sacred space of land, temple, and cult as ancient Near Eastern worldview
demands.[36]

As Ronald Simkins observes of other ANE creation texts:

---

[35] See also Psa. 77:16-20; 136:1-22.
[36] N.T. Wright, *The New Testament and the People of God* (Minneapolis, MN: Fortress Press, 1992), 306-307.

"According to the *Enuma Elish*, for example, Marduk chose Babylon to be the special place of his temple and organized the rest of the creation around it. In the [Sumerian] *Creation of the Pickax* humans sprout from the ground at Uzumua, and Duranki is the place at which heaven and earth were originally attached. In the Egyptian creation myths, the land of Egypt is the hillock that first emerged out of the primeval ocean Nun…Each place is a symbolic geographical expression of the structure of creation…The ideas of creation and the experiences of sacred space are mutually dependent."[37]

This "covenant as creation" word picture is reiterated in a negative way when God judges nations and cultures. If creation of covenant involved establishing the foundations of the heavens and the earth, then covenantal judgment involves "decreation" imagery of the destruction or "shaking" of heavens and earth. Haggai conveys this decreation polemic against the nations:

"Then the word of the Lord came a second time to Haggai… saying, "Speak to Zerubbabel governor of Judah, saying, 'I am going to shake the heavens and the earth.' I will overthrow the thrones of kingdoms and destroy the power of the kingdoms of the nations" (Hag. 2:20-22).

Jeremiah calls the destruction of Jerusalem in 587 B.C. a return of the heavens and earth to the "formless and void" (*tohu wabohu*) of Genesis 1:2 without man or beast yet created[38]:

"I looked on the earth, and behold, it was formless and void; And to the heavens, and they had no light. I looked on the mountains, and behold, they were quaking, And all the hills moved to and fro. I looked, and behold, there was no man,

---

[37] Simkins, *Creator and Creation*, 133.
[38] David Chilton, *The Days of Vengeance: An Exposition of the Book of Revelation* (Ft. Worth, TX: Dominion Press,1987-1990), 541.

And all the birds of the heavens had fled. I looked, and behold, the fruitful land was a wilderness" (Jer. 4:23-27).

Isaiah proclaims the "good news" of a New Covenant in Messiah (Isa. 61) as a "new heavens and a new earth" (Isa. 65).[39] Covenant is understood as creation of a heaven and earth, so important covenantal events, such as judgment on a people or creation of a new covenant, are understood as shaking that heaven and earth or a return to a pre-creation state of the universe.

The New Covenant kingdom as a "new heavens and earth" is picked up in the New Testament with the same language of shaking and removing of the previous heavens and earth:

"Yet once more I will shake not only the earth, but also the heaven." And this expression, "Yet once more," denotes the removing of those things which can be shaken, as of created things, in order that those things which cannot be shaken may remain. *Therefore, since we receive a kingdom which cannot be shaken* [emphasis added]..." (Heb. 12:26-28).

The replacement of the Old Covenant of Moses with the New Covenant of Christ is here described as God "shaking" and "removing" the old heavens and earth.[40] To the ancient Jew, the covenants of God with His people are the very "cosmos" of their existence and meaning. So important covenantal events are described in cosmic terms, and the purpose of creation language is theological not natural or "scientific."

The inauguration of the New Covenant through the incarnation of Christ is reaffirmed in Revelation as a new heaven and earth cosmos coming out of heaven to eliminate chaos (the sea) and bring a new sacred space of holy city and temple fulfilled in Christ[41]:

---

[39] John Calvin, *Commentary on the Book of the Prophet Isaiah*, Trans William Pringle (Grand Rapids, MI: Eerdmans, 1948), 4:397-398.
[40] Kenneth L. Gentry, Jr., *He Shall Have Dominion: A Postmillennial Eschatology* (Draper, VA: Apologetics Group Media, 1992, 2009), 259.
[41] Kenneth L. Gentry, Jr., *Navigating the Book of Revelation: Special Studies on Important Issues* (Fountain Inn, SC: GoodBirth Ministries, 2009), 167-174;

"Then I saw a new heaven and a new earth; for the first heaven and the first earth passed away, and there is no longer any sea. And I saw the holy city, new Jerusalem, coming down out of heaven from God, made ready as a bride adorned for her husband. And I heard a loud voice from the throne, saying, "Behold, the tabernacle of God is among men, and He will dwell among them, and they shall be His people, and God Himself will be among them" (Rev. 21:1-3).[42]

Conclusion

A *merism* is a phrase of joined opposites that indicate a totality. The Hebrew for "heavens and earth" has long been accepted as a merism of the ordered cosmos.[43] Whereas the modern scientific mind conceives of "cosmos" as a physical system of materials and their properties, the ancient Near Eastern mind of the Hebrew conceived of "cosmos" as the covenantal order of God. Everything had its place and purpose in God's plan for His people in their land. The idea of the earth as a spherical globe and the heavens as a vast expanse of light years was alien to their thinking. As noted expert on Biblical apocalyptics, Milton Terry wrote, "In these opening chapters of Genesis we are not to look for historic narrative, nor contributions to natural science, but to recognize a symbolic apocalypse of God's relation to the world and to man."[44]

John Sailhamer makes the connection between covenant and creation in arguing that God's preparation of the Edenic Garden in Genesis is a parallel to His preparation of the Promised Land in Deuteronomy, because in fact,

---

[42] That this passage depicts the inauguration of the New Covenant with the incarnation of Christ rather than a future event at Christ's "Second Coming," is evident in a couple of observations. First, the reference to God dwelling with tabernacle among men is well understood as a theological expression of the incarnation in John 1:14 "And the Word became flesh, and dwelt (*tabernacled*) among us." Secondly, a heavenly Jerusalem coming down from above is previewed in the Hebrews 12:18-24 description of the New Covenant as the "heavenly Jerusalem," in comparison with the Old Covenant of an earthly Jerusalem; and that New Covenant is reiterated by the apostle Paul in Galatians 4:24-26 as the "Jerusalem from above." Also, the body of Christ is the bride of Christ, which constitutes the new temple of God (Eph 2:19-22).

[43] Bruce Waltke, *Genesis: A Commentary* (Grand Rapids, MI: Zondervan, 2001), 59.

[44] Milton Terry, *Biblical Apocalyptics: A Study of the Most Notable Revelations of God and of Christ* (Grand Rapids, MI: Baker Books, 1898, 1988), 49.

they are the same exact location!; "Heavens and earth" is not about a globe and solar systems, but about a more localized "sky and land"; "Formless and void" (*tohu wabohu*) is better translated "wilderness and uninhabitable," a term applied to the Promised Land without God's blessing (Jer. 4:23); "working" and "keeping" (*abad* and *shamar*) the Garden of God's presence (Gen. 2:15) is more suitably translated as "worshipping and obeying" in a parallel of the Tabernacle of God.[45] Sailhamer concludes that the covenant on Sinai is grounded in the events of creation. "The writer of the Pentateuch wrote Genesis 1 primarily because he wanted his readers to understand something about God and the nature of the covenant He made with Israel on Mt. Sinai... Thus, the theme of the Sinai Covenant — God's good gift of the promised land — lies at the center of the author's account of creation."[46]

The Bible is covenantal storytelling in theme and structure. The purpose of the exalted prose of Genesis 1 seems to be covenantal justification of Yahweh's ownership of everything, specifically the Promised Land He was about to forcibly take from the Canaanites and give to Israel. *Chaoskampf* poetry of subduing the Sea and the twisting serpent or dragon Leviathan/Rahab is metaphorically united with creation language. That creation language is often used to narrate the covenantal order of Israel while decreation language is used to narrate covenantal disorder. The localized ancient Near Eastern mindset of the text of Genesis revealing purpose through naming, separating, and giving function does not comport with a modern post-Enlightenment scientific mindset of astrophysics and material substance and properties. One can only conclude that the attempt to find a concordance between Genesis 1 and any kind of scientific theory, be it young-earth or old-earth, 24 hour days or long ages, fiat creation or evolutionary adaptation is an act of interpretive violence against the text that comes from a culturally imposing modern hubris.

---

[45] John Sailhamer, *Genesis Unbound: A Provocative New Look at the Creation Account* (Sisters, OR: Multnomah, 1996), 47-59, 61-66, 75-76.
[46] Sailhamer, *Genesis Unbound*, 87-88.

CHAPTER 4

The Universe in Ancient Imagination

This chapter has been adapted from "Appendix D: Mesopotamian Cosmic Geography in the Bible" in the novel Noah Primeval.

Cosmography is a technical term that means a theory that describes and maps the main features of the heavens and the earth. A cosmography or "cosmic geography" can be a complex picture of the universe that includes elements like astronomy, geology, and geography; and those elements can include theological implications as well. Throughout history, all civilizations and peoples operate under the assumption of a cosmography or picture of the universe. We are most familiar with the historical change that science went through from a Ptolemaic cosmography of the earth at the center of the universe (geocentrism) to a Copernican cosmography of the sun at the center of a galaxy (heliocentrism).

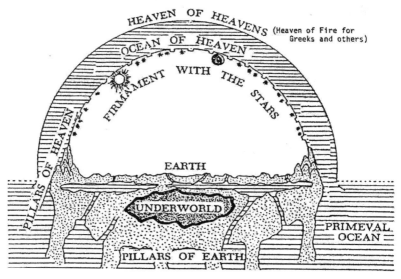

This antique drawing represents the Mesopotamian picture of the universe used in this story.

Some mythologies maintained that the earth was a flat disc on the back of a giant turtle; animistic cultures believe that spirits inhabit natural objects and cause them to behave in certain ways; modern westerners believe in a space-time continuum where everything is relative to its frame of reference in relation to the speed of light. Ancients tended to believe that the gods caused the weather; moderns tend to believe that impersonal physical processes cause weather. All these different beliefs are elements of a cosmography or picture of what the universe is really like and how it operates. Even though "pre-scientific" cultures like the ancient Jews did not have the same notions of science that we moderns have, they still observed the world around them and made interpretations as to the structure and operations of the universe.

A common ancient understanding of this cosmos is expressed in the visions of 1 Enoch. In this Second Temple Jewish writing, codified around the third to fourth century B.C., and most likely written much earlier, Enoch is taken on a journey through heaven and hell and describes the cosmic workings as they understood them in that day. Here is just a short glimpse into the elaborate construction of this ANE author:

1 Enoch 18:1-5
And I saw the storerooms of all the winds and saw how with them he has embroidered all creation as well as the foundations of the earth. I saw the cornerstone of the earth; I saw the four winds which bear the earth as well as the firmament of heaven. I saw how the winds ride the heights of heaven and stand between heaven and earth: These are the very pillars of heaven. I saw the winds which turn the heaven and cause the star to set — the sun as well as all the stars. I saw the souls carried by the clouds. I saw the path of the angels in the ultimate end of the earth, and the firmament of the heaven above.[1]

---

[1] James H. Charlesworth, *The Old Testament Pseudepigrapha: Volume 1*, 1 En 18 (New York; London: Yale University Press, 1983).

I am not a scientist, I am a professional storyteller, and so my interest in Biblical cosmography comes from my study of imagery, metaphor, and story. But a picture of the cosmos certainly has a bearing on scientific notions of the way the universe is and operates. Imagination and science are not completely unconnected. I am also a Christian who believes that the Bible is the Word of God. But does this mean that the Bible will have a cosmography that agrees with modern western science? I used to believe it did. I used to believe that if the Bible was scientifically "wrong" in anyway, then it could not be the Word of God, since God would never communicate false information to us. That would make God a liar.

This led to the corollary that whatever modern science discovered could not contradict the Bible. This is called "scientific concordism," and it is the attempt to bring our knowledge of natural revelation *in accord* with our interpretation of special revelation. So, if we now know that the earth is a sphere and that the universe is expanding, then Scripture would not contradict that truth. What's more, I might even be able to find a verse that would have that truth hidden in it. Behold, I thought I found it: "It is He who sits above the circle of the earth...who stretches out the heavens like a curtain" (Isa. 40:22). In this scientific concordist paradigm, the Bible contains veiled scientific truths before their time in a gnostic hiddenness that is uncovered by modern initiates into such mysteries.

Unfortunately, this paradigm would lead to much cognitive dissonance for me as I tortured the text to fit whatever scientific theory I was trying to support at the time. First, I accepted Genesis as literally explaining material creation chronology and relegated evolutionary scientists to dishonest manipulators of facts.[2] Then I tried to find dinosaurs in the Bible by interpreting the Leviathan or Behemoth as references to ichthyosaurs and

---

[2] I never believed they were all lying, but many were certainly blinded by their worldview bias. I still believe that some scientists do in fact lie, cheat, and manipulate facts and studies just as in every other discipline because they are human like everyone else and can be just as driven by political and personal agenda as everyone else. A good book that documents this is *Betrayers Of The Truth: Fraud And Deceit In The Halls Of Science* By Nicholas Wade William Broad (Ebury Press, 1983); Michael Fumento is a science journalist who reports on current scientific fraud and its widespread economic and political effects at www.fumento.com.

sauropods.[3] Then I tried to make six literal days and young chronology of Creation in Genesis square symbolically with the seriously old age of the earth.[4] Then I tried to creatively reconcile the billions of years of the Big Bang with 24-hour earth-bound solar days though gravity-warped space-time.[5]

I also thought that the best interpretation of the Bible was the "plain reading" of the text. That is, any interpretation that would turn the meaning into unwarranted figurative, symbolic, allegorical or metaphorical language would be disingenuous hermeneutics. I didn't mean obvious figurative and allegorical language like parables of talking brambles and trees (Judg. 9:7-15) or clearly poetic expressions of singing mountains and clapping trees (Isa. 55:12). I meant that when the Bible talked about the physical order and events in heaven and earth it would mean just what it said since the Creator of the cosmos would know best what was actually happening.

But something started to seriously challenge these assumptions. First, as I studied the ancient Hebrew culture and its surrounding Near Eastern background, I began to see how very different a "plain reading" of a text was to them than a "plain reading" was to me.[6] The ancient Hebrew mind was steeped in different symbols, ideas, and language than I was. If I read a phrase like "sun, moon and stars," my western cultural understanding, which is deeply affected by a post-Galileo, post-Enlightened, materialist science would tend to read such references in terms of the physical bodies of matter, gas, and gravity spread out over vast light years of space-time. When ancient Israelites used that phrase, they would have pictures in their minds of markers and signs (Gen. 1:14), and more personal objects like pagan gods

---

[3] *Scientific Creationism* by Henry M. Morris (Master Books, 1974, 1985) is an example of this viewpoint.

[4] *Creation and Time: A Biblical and Scientific Perspective on the Creation-Date Controversy* by Hugh Ross (NavPress, 1994) is an example of this viewpoint.

[5] *Genesis and the Big Bang: The Discovery Of Harmony Between Modern Science And The Bible* by Gerald Schroeder (Bantam, 1990) is an example of this viewpoint.

[6] The seminal book that opened the door for me to a better understanding of this ANE cultural context of the Bible was John H. Walton, *Ancient Near Eastern Thought and the Old Testament: Introducing the Conceptual World of the Hebrew Bible* (Grand Rapids, MI: Baker, 2006).

(Deut. 4:19), heavenly beings (1 Kgs. 22:19), symbolic influential leaders (Gen. 37:9), or the fall of governing powers (Isa. 13:10).[7]

An ancient Jew hearing the words *leviathan* and *sea* conjured up notions of a disordered world without Yahweh's rule, and Yahweh's covenant creation out of chaos.[8] Whereas for me, hearing those words makes me think of a monster fish swimming in the ocean — or maybe *Moby Dick*, a symbol of man's hubris — but primarily the physical material being of those objects. It is easier to see now that my plain reading of the text through my modern western worldview could completely miss the plain meaning that the Scripture would have to an ancient Israelite. My so-called act of "plain reading" was ironically an imposition of my own cultural bias onto the text removed by thousands of years, thousands of miles, and thousands of cultural motifs.[9] We must seek the "plain reading" *of the ancient authors and their audience*, and in this way we can be "diligent to present yourself approved to God as a workman who does not need to be ashamed, accurately handling the word of truth" (2 Tim. 2:15).

Something else had always haunted me like a nagging pebble in the shoe of my mind, and that was the Galileo affair. There was a time (the 17th century) when brilliant godly Christian theologians and scientists that I greatly respect considered the new heliocentric theory as being against the plain teaching of the Bible. They believed the Bible could not be wrong about the way the cosmos operated without jeopardizing its authority as the Word of God. They asserted that the Bible plainly says *in clear and unambiguous language* that the earth does not move (Psa. 93:1; 104:5) and that the sun goes around the earth (Josh. 10:13; Eccl. 1:5).[10] These were

---

[7] "The worship of the host of heaven [was] often set in parallelism to the worship of foreign gods (Deut. 17:3; 2 Kgs. 17:16; 21:3; 23:4–5; Jer. 19:13; Zeph. 1:4–5)." K. van der Toorn, Bob Becking and Pieter Willem van der Horst, *Dictionary of Deities and Demons in the Bible DDD*, 2nd extensively rev. ed., 429 (Leiden; Boston; Grand Rapids, Mich.: Brill; Eerdmans, 1999), 429.

[8] Brian Godawa, "Biblical Creation and Storytelling: Cosmogony, Combat and Covenant," The BioLogos Foundation, http://biologos.org/uploads/projects/godawa_scholarly_paper.pdf.

[9] Othmar Keel's *The Symbolism of the Biblical World* (Eisenbrauns) is an encyclopedia of imagery and motifs that Israel shared with her ANE neighbors that are quite alien to our thinking.

[10] In *John Calvin's Commentary on the Book of Psalms*, Psa. 93:1, Psa. 104:5-6 he affirms the Ptolemaic notion in Scripture. See "Calvin and the Astronomical Revolution" Matthew F. Dowd, University of Notre Dame: http://www.nd.edu/~mdowd1/postings/CalvinAstroRev.html accessed March 21, 2011

brilliant men and not the ignorant anti-scientific bigots that they are still portrayed to be by critics with an axe to grind. They eventually accepted the theory as the evidence came in to back it up. But the point was that they learned a principle that has far reaching implications in Bible interpretation (hermeneutics): *Sometimes science can correct our interpretation of the Bible.*

There it is, I said it. A statement that draws the ire of Evangelicals who automatically accuse you of being a "liberal" and of not believing the Bible. But the fact of history is that science *has* corrected that very Evangelical tradition of interpreting of the Bible. I really hated to admit this too, because I believe that the Bible is my ultimate authority on the truth of God, so if science could correct the Bible, then would that not make science a higher authority than the Bible? Only if you assume that your *interpretation of the Bible* is exactly what God is trying to communicate to you. But our *interpretation* of God's intent and meaning is not always the same thing as God's *actual* intent and meaning. So revising our understanding of the meaning of God's Word does not make God's Word wrong, but rather it makes our *interpretation* of God's Word wrong *by showing us that we are expecting of the Scriptures something that the Scriptures are not offering us.*

The implications of this principle forced me to re-evaluate my own understanding of just what the Bible is saying when it comes to science and cosmography. Because of my modern western scientific bias, I could easily misinterpret something as literal that was intended to be figurative, such as stars falling from the sky and the sun and moon losing their light (Isa. 13:10; Ezek. 32:7; Matt. 24:29).[11] But I also realized something just as important: My modern western scientific bias could also guide me to misinterpret something as figurative that the Bible intended to be literal! If I read about the "floodgates of heaven" for rain (Gen. 7:11), or the earth set upon a foundation of pillars (Psa. 75:3) or of Sheol being below the earth (Num. 13:32-33), I automatically think of these as poetic metaphors because

---

[11] N.T. Wright, *Jesus and the Victory of God* (Minneapolis: Fortress, 1996), p. 320-367. For more biblical examples of this collapsing universe and earth shattering hyperbole used of the fall of worldly powers see Jer. 4:23-30; Amos 8:9; Isa. 24:1-23; 40:3-5; Nah. 1:4-6. For an excellent book about the nature of this apocalyptic imagery and symbolism in the Bible, a must-buy book is *Last Days Madness*, by Gary DeMar, Powder Springs, GA: American Vision, 1999.

modern science has revealed that none of these things are "literally" or physically there. But the ancient Israelite did not know these scientific facts that I know now, so what did these images mean to them?

The Bible also contains a picture of the universe that its stories inhabit. It uses cosmic geographical language in common with other ancient Near Eastern cultures that shared its situated time and location. Believers in today's world use the language of Relativity when we write, even in our non-scientific discourse; because Einstein has affected the way they see the universe. Christians before the 17th century used Ptolemaic language because they too were children of their time. It should be no surprise to anyone that believers in ancient Israel would use the language of ANE cosmography because it was the mental construct within which they lived and thought.[12]

The Three-Tiered Universe

Othmar Keel, leading expert on ANE art has argued that there was no singular technical physical description of the cosmos in the ancient Near East, but rather patterns of thinking, similarity of images, and repetition of motifs.[13] But a common simplification of these images and motifs is expressed in the three-tiered universe of the heavens, the earth, and the underworld.

Wayne Horowitz has chronicled Mesopotamian texts that illustrate this multi-leveled universe among the successive civilizations of Sumer, Akkad, Babylonia, and Assyria. The heavens above were subdivided into "the heaven of Anu (or chief god)" at the very top, the "middle heavens" below him and the sky. In the middle was the earth's surface, and below that was the third level that was further divided into the waters of the abyss and the underworld.[14] The generalized version of this was "heaven, earth, and under the earth."

---

[12] The book that opened my mind to the Mesopotamian cosmography in the Bible was *Evolutionary Creation: A Christian Approach to Evolution* by Denis O. Lamoureux, Eugene; OR, Wipf & Stock, 2008. I owe much of the material in this essay to Mr. Lamoureux's meticulous research on the ancient science in the Bible.

[13] Othmar Keel, *The Symbolism of the Biblical World*, Winona Lake; IN: Eisenbrauns, 1972, 1997, 16-59.

[14] Wayne Horowitz, *Mesopotamian Cosmic Geography*, Winona Lake; IN: Eisenbrauns, 1998, xii-xiii.

Let's take a look at the Scriptures that appear to reinforce this three-tiered universe so different from our modern understanding of physical expanding galaxies of warped space-time, where the notion of heaven and hell are without physical location. Though the focus of this essay will be on Old Testament context, I want to start with the New Testament to make the point that their cosmography did not necessarily change with the change of Old to New Covenants.

> Phil. 2:10
> That at the name of Jesus every knee should bow, <u>in heaven</u>, and <u>on earth</u>, and <u>under the earth</u>.

> Rev. 5:3, 13
> And no one <u>in heaven, or on earth, or under the earth</u>, was able to open the scroll, or to look into it... And every creature <u>in heaven and on the earth and under the earth</u> and in the sea, and all that is in them, saying,
> "To Him who sits on the throne and to the Lamb
> be blessing and honor and glory and might forever and ever!"

> Exod. 20:4
> "You shall not make for yourself a carved image, or any likeness of anything that is in <u>heaven above,</u> or that is <u>in the earth beneath</u>, or that is in the <u>water under the earth</u>.

> Matt. 11:23
> Jesus said, "Capernaum, will you be <u>exalted to heaven</u>? You will be <u>brought down to Hades</u>. [the underworld].

Both apostles Paul and John were writing about the totality of creation being subject to the authority of Jesus on His throne. So this word picture of "heaven, earth, and under the earth" was used as the description of the total known universe — which they conceived of spatially as heaven above, the earth below, and the underworld below the earth. And not only did the inspired human authors write of the universe in this three-tiered fashion but so did God Himself, the author and finisher of our faith, when giving the commandments on Sinai.

One may naturally wonder if this notion of "heaven above" may merely be a symbolic or figurative expression for the exalted spiritual nature of heaven. Since we cannot see where heaven is, God would use physical analogies to express spiritual truths. This explanation would be easier to stomach if the three-tiered notion were not so rooted in a cosmic geography that clearly was their understanding of the universe (as proven below). A figurative expression would also jeopardize the doctrine of the ascension of Jesus into heaven which also affirms the spatial location of heaven above and the earth below, in very literal terms.

> Acts 1:9-11
> He was lifted up, and a cloud took Him out of their sight. And while they were gazing <u>into heaven</u> as he went, behold, two men stood by them in white robes, and said, "Men of Galilee, why do you stand looking <u>into heaven</u>? This Jesus, who was <u>taken up from you into heaven</u>, will come in the same way as you saw Him go <u>into heaven</u>."

> John 3:13
> No one has <u>ascended into heaven</u> except He who <u>descended from heaven</u>, the Son of Man.

> John 6:62
> Then what if you were to see the <u>Son of Man ascending</u> to where He was before?

> John 20:17
> Jesus said to her, "Do not cling to me, for I have not yet <u>ascended to the Father</u>; but go to my brothers and say to them, 'I am <u>ascending to my Father</u> and your Father, to my God and your God.'"

Eph. 4:8-10

Therefore it says, "When <u>He ascended on high</u> He led a host of captives, and He gave gifts to men." (In saying, "<u>He ascended</u>," what does it mean but that <u>He had also descended into the lower regions, the earth</u>? He who <u>descended is the one who also ascended far above all the heavens</u>, that He might fill all things.)

The location of heaven being above us may be figurative to our modern cosmology, but it was not figurative to the Biblical writers. To suggest that they understood it figuratively would be to impose our own modern cultural bias on the Bible. That is what we call *cultural imperialism*. It marks the inability to see outside of one's own perception and understand others.

Now let's take a closer look at each of these tiers or domains of the cosmos through the eyes of Scripture in their ANE context.

Flat Earth Surrounded by Waters

I want to start with the earth because the Scriptures start with the earth. That is, the Bible is geocentric in its picture of a flat earth founded on immovable pillars at the center of the universe. Over a hundred years ago, a Babylonian map of the world was discovered that dated back to approximately the ninth century B.C. As seen below, this map was unique from other Mesopotamian maps because it was not merely local but international in its scale, and contained features that appeared to indicate cosmological interpretation.[15] That map and a translated interpretation are reproduced below.[16]

---

[15] Horowitz, *Mesopotamian Cosmic Geography*, 25-27.
[16] Photo is public domain (Courtesy of the British Museum). Illustration is my own based on Horowitz, *Mesopotamian Cosmic Geography*, 21.

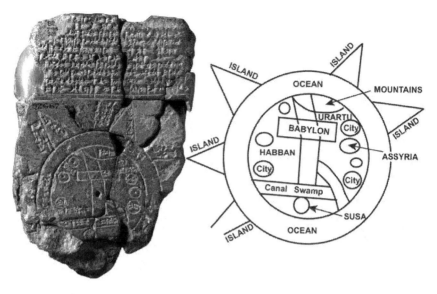

The geography of the Babylonian map portrayed a flat disc of earth with Babylon in the center and extending out to the known regions of its empire, whose perimeters were surrounded by cosmic waters and islands out in those waters. Of the earliest Sumerian and Akkadian texts with geographical information, only the Babylonian map of the world and another text, *The Sargon Geography,* describe the earth's surface, and they both picture a central circular flat continent surrounded by cosmic waters, often referred to as "the circle of the earth."[17] Other texts like the Akkadian *Epic of Gilgamesh,* and Egyptian and Sumerian works share in common with the Babylonian map the notion of mountains at the edge of the earth beyond which is the cosmic sea and the unknown,[18] and from which come "the circle

---

[17] Horowitz, *Mesopotamian Cosmic Geography*, 320, 334. This interpretation continued to maintain influence even into the Greek period of the 6th century B.C. (41).

[18] A Sumerian hymn to the god Enlil, Lord of the Wind, represents these ends of the earth within the context of the god's rule over all the earth:

Lord, as far as the edge of heaven, lord as far as the edge of earth, from the mountain of sunrise to the mountain of sunset. In the mountain/land, no (other) lord resides, you exercise lordship. Enlil, in the lands no (other) lady resides, your wife, exercises ladyship. Horowitz, *Mesopotamian Cosmic Geography*, 331.

"Circle of the earth" in Egyptian understanding meant the disc of the earth unto the horizon "(These) lands were united, and they laid their hands upon the land as far as the Circle of the Earth." "Inscription on the second pylon at Medinet Habu," J.H. Breasted, *Ancient Records of Egypt*, Part Four, University of Chicago, 1906, p 64.

of the four winds" that blow upon the four corners of the earth (a reference to compass points).[19]

The Biblical picture of the earth is remarkably similar to this Mesopotamian cosmic geography. When Daniel had his dream *from God in Babylon*, of a tree "in the middle of the earth" whose height reached so high that "it was visible to the end of the whole earth," (Dan. 4:10) it reflected this very Babylonian map of the culture that educated Daniel. One cannot see the end of the whole earth on a globe, but one can do so on a circular continent embodying the known world of Babylon as the center of the earth.

"The ends of the earth" is a common phrase, occurring over fifty times throughout the Scriptures that means more than just "remote lands," but rather includes the notion of the very physical end of the whole earth all around before the cosmic waters that hem it in. Here are just a few of the verses that indicate this circular land mass bounded by seas as the entire earth:

> Isa. 41:9
> You whom I took from the ends of the earth, and called from its farthest corners...

> Psa. 65:5
> O God of our salvation, the hope of all the ends of the earth and of the farthest seas...

> Zech. 9:10
> His rule shall be from sea to sea, and from the River to the ends of the earth.

> Mark 13:27
> And then He will send out the angels and gather His elect from the four winds, from the ends of the earth to the ends of heaven.

---

[19] Horowitz, *Mesopotamian Cosmic Geography*, 195-97, 334.

Acts 13:47
'I have made you a light for the Gentiles, that you may bring salvation to the ends of the earth.'

Job 28:24
For He looks to the ends of the earth and sees everything under the heavens.

Remember that Mesopotamian phrase, "circle of the earth" that meant a flat disc terra firma? Well, it's in the Bible, too. "It is He who sits above the circle of the earth, and its inhabitants are like grasshoppers" (Isa. 40:22). Some have tried to say that the Hebrew word for "circle" could mean *sphere*, but it does not. The Hebrew word used here (*ḥûg*) could however refer to a vaulted dome that covers the visible circular horizon, which would be more accurate to say, "above the vault of the earth."[20] If Isaiah had wanted to say the earth was a sphere he would have used another word that he used in a previous chapter (22:18) for a ball, but he did not.[21]

Two further Scriptures use this "circle of the earth" in reference to God's original creation of the land out of the waters and extend it outward to include the circumferential ocean with its own mysterious boundary:

Prov. 8:27, 29
When He established the heavens, I was there; when He drew a circle on the face of the deep... when He assigned to the sea its limit, so that the waters might not transgress His command, when He marked out the foundations of the earth.

---

[20] "*ḥûg*" Harris, R. Laird, Robert Laird Harris, Gleason Leonard Archer, and Bruce K. Waltke. *Theological Wordbook of the Old Testament*. electronic ed. Chicago: Moody Press, 1999, p 266-67.

[21] Even the Septuagint (LXX) does not translate the Hebrew word into the Greek word for sphere. "Isaiah 40:22," Tan, Randall, David A. deSilva, and Logos Bible Software. *The Lexham Greek-English Interlinear Septuagint*. Logos Bible Software, 2009.

Job 26:10

He has inscribed a circle on the face of the waters at the boundary between light and darkness [where the sun rises and sets].

Even when the Old Testament writers are deliberately using metaphors for the earth, they use metaphors for a flat earth spread out like a flat blanket.

Job 38:13

Take hold of the skirts of the earth, and the wicked be shaken out of it.

Job 38:18

Have you comprehended the expanse of the earth?

Psa. 136:6

To Him who spreads out the earth above the waters.

Isa. 44:24

"I am the LORD, who spread out the earth by myself."

Geocentricity

In the Bible, the earth is not merely a flat disk surrounded by cosmic waters under the heavens; it is also the center of the universe. To the ANE mindset, including that of the Hebrews, the earth did not move (except for earthquakes) and the sun revolved around that immovable earth. They did not know that the earth was spinning one thousand miles an hour and flying through space at 65,000 miles an hour. Evidently, God did not consider it important enough to correct this primitive inaccurate understanding. Here are the passages that caused such trouble with Christians who took the text too literally because it did not seem to be figurative to them:

Psa. 19:4-6

Their voice goes out through all the earth,

and their words to <u>the end of the world</u>.
In them He has set a tent for the sun,
which comes out like a bridegroom leaving His chamber,
and, like a strong man, <u>runs its course</u> with joy.
Its rising is from the end of the heavens,
and its circuit to the end of them.

Psa. 50:1
The Mighty One, God, the LORD, speaks and summons the
earth from <u>the rising of the sun to its setting</u>.

Eccl. 1:5
The sun rises, and the sun goes down,
and hastens to the place where it rises.

Josh. 10:13
And the sun stood still, and the moon stopped,
until the nation took vengeance on their enemies…
<u>The sun stopped in the midst of heaven</u> and did not hurry to
set for about a whole day.

Matt. 5:45
Jesus said, "For He makes His <u>sun rise</u> on the evil and on the
good."

Before the Copernican Revolution, Christians took the "plain reading"
of the text to mean that the sun clearly goes around the stationary earth. Two
objections are often raised when considering these passages. First, that they
use phenomenal language. That is, they describe simply what the viewer
observes and makes no cosmological claims beyond simply description of
what one sees. We even use these terms of the sun rising and setting today
and we know the earth moves around the sun. Fair enough. The only
problem is that the ancient writers were pre-scientific and did not know the
earth went around the sun, so when they said the sun was moving from one
end of the heavens to the other they believed reality was exactly as they

observed it. They had absolutely no reason to believe in a "phenomenal distinction" between their observation and reality.[22]

The second objection is that some of the language is obvious metaphor. David painted the sun as a bridegroom coming out of his chamber or of being summoned by God and responding like a human. This is called anthropomorphism and is obviously poetic. But the problem here is that the metaphors still reinforce the sun doing all the moving around a stationary immobile earth.

> 1 Chr. 16:30
> Tremble before Him, all the earth;
> yes, the world is established; <u>it shall never be moved</u>.

> Psa. 93:1
> Yes, the world is established; <u>it shall never be moved</u>.

> Psa. 96:10
> Yes, the world is established; <u>it shall never be moved</u>;

Understandably, these texts have been thought to indicate that the Bible is explicitly saying the earth does not move. But the case is not so strong for these examples because the Hebrew word used in these passages for "the world" is not the word for *earth* (*erets*), but the word that is sometimes used for the inhabited world (*tebel*). So it is possible that these verses are talking about the "the world order" as does the poetry of 2 Sam. 22:16.

But the problem that then arises is that the broader chapter context of these verses describe the earth's physical aspects such as oceans, trees, and in the case of 1 Chron. 16:30, even the "earth" (*erets*) in redundant context with the "world" (*tebel*), which would seem to indicate that "world" may indeed refer to the physical earth.

Lastly, *world* can be interchangeable with *earth* as it is in 1 Sam. 2:8, "For the pillars of <u>the earth</u> are the LORD'S, And He set <u>the world</u> on them."

---

[22] "The Firmament And The Water Above: Part I: The Meaning Of Raqia In Gen 1:6-8," Paul H. Seely, *The Westminster Theological Journal* 53 (1991) 227-40.

And this adds a new element to the conversation of a stationary earth: *A foundation of pillars*.

Pillars of the Earth

The notion of an immovable earth is not a mere description of observational experience by earth dwellers; it is based upon another cosmographical notion that the earth is on a foundation of pillars that hold it firmly in place.

> Psa. 104:5
> He set the <u>earth on its foundations</u>, so that it should never be moved.

> Job 38:4
> "Where were you when I laid <u>the foundation of the earth</u>? Tell Me, if you have understanding, Who <u>set its measurements</u>, since you know? Or who <u>stretched the line</u> on it? "On what were <u>its bases sunk</u>? Or who <u>laid its cornerstone</u>,

> 2 Sam. 22:16
> "Then the channels of the sea were seen; <u>the foundations of the world were laid bare</u>, at the rebuke of the LORD, At the blast of the breath of His nostrils.

> 1 Sam. 2:8
> For the <u>pillars of the earth</u> are the LORD's, and on them, <u>He has set the world</u>.

> Psa. 75:3
> "When <u>the earth totters</u>, and all its inhabitants,
> it is I who keep steady its pillars.

Zech. 12:1
Thus declares the LORD who stretches out the heavens, <u>and founded the earth.</u>

Ancient man such as the Babylonians believed that mountains and important ziggurat temples had foundations that went below the earth into the abyss (*apsu*) or the underworld.[23] But even if one would argue that the notion of foundations and pillars of the earth are only intended to be symbolic, they are still symbolic *of a stationary earth that does not move.*

Some have pointed out the single verse that seems to mitigate this notion of a solid foundation of pillars, Job 26:6-7: "Sheol is naked before God, and Abaddon has no covering. He stretches out the north over the void and <u>hangs the earth on nothing</u>." They suggest that this is a revelation of the earth in space before ancient man even knew about the spatial location of the earth in a galaxy. But the reason I do not believe this is because of the context of the verse.

Within chapter 26 Job affirms the three-tiered universe of waters of the Abyss below him (v. 5) and under that Sheol (v. 6), with pillars holding up the heavens (v. 11). Later in the same book, God Himself speaks about the earth laid on foundations (38:4), sinking its bases and cornerstone like a building (38:5-6). Ancient peoples believed the earth was on top of some other object like the back of a turtle, and that it was too heavy to float on the waters. So in context, Job 26 appears to be saying that the earth is over the waters of the abyss and Sheol, on its foundations, but there is nothing under *those pillars* but God Himself holding it all up. This is not the suggestion of a planet hanging in space, but rather the negative claim of an earth that is *not* on the back of a turtle or other ancient object.

Sheol Below

Before we ascend to the heavens, let's take a look at the Underworld below the earth. The Underworld was a common location of extensive stories about gods and departed souls of men journeying to the depths of the

---

[23] Horowitz, *Mesopotamian Cosmic Geography*, 98, 124, 308-12, 336-37.

earth through special gates of some kind into a geographic location that might also be accessed through cracks in the earth above.[24] Entire Mesopotamian stories engage the location of the subterranean netherworld in their narrative such as *The Descent of Inanna, The Descent of Ishtar, Nergal and Ereshkigal,* and many others.

Sheol was the Hebrew word for the underworld.[25] Though the Bible does not contain any narratives of experiences in Sheol, it was nevertheless described as the abode of the dead that was below the earth. Though Sheol was sometimes used interchangeably with "Abaddon" as the place of destruction of the body (Prov. 15:11; 27:20),[26] and "the grave" (*qibrah*) as a reference to the state of being dead and buried in the earth (Psa. 88:11; Isa. 14:9-11) it was also considered to be *physically* located beneath the earth in the same way as other ANE worldviews.

When the sons of Korah are swallowed up by the earth for their rebellion against God, Numbers chapter 16 says that "they <u>went down alive into Sheol</u>, and the earth closed over them, and they perished from the midst of the assembly (v. 33)." People would not "fall alive" into death or the grave and then perish if Sheol was not a location. But they would die after they fall down into a location (Sheol) and the earth closes over them in that order.

The divine being (*elohim*), known as the departed spirit of Samuel, "came up out of the earth" for the witch of Endor's necromancy with Saul (1 Sam. 28:13). This was not a reference to a body coming out of a grave, but a spirit of the dead coming from a location beneath the earth.

When Isaiah writes about Sheol in Isaiah 14, he combines the notion of the physical location of the dead body in the earth (v. 11) with the location beneath the earth of the spirits of the dead (v. 9). It's really a both/and proposition.

Here is a list of some verses that speak of Sheol geographically as a spiritual underworld in contrast with heaven as a spatially located spiritual overworld.

---

[24] Horowitz, *Mesopotamian Cosmic Geography*, p 348-362
[25] "Sheol," *DDD*, p 768.
[26] "Abaddon," *DDD*, p 1.

Amos 9:2

"If they <u>dig into Sheol</u>, from there shall my hand take them;
if they climb <u>up to heaven</u>, from there I will bring them
down.

Job 11:8

It is <u>higher than heaven</u>—what can you do? <u>Deeper than
Sheol</u>—what can you know?

Psa. 16:10

For you will not abandon <u>my soul</u> to Sheol, or let your holy
one <u>see corruption</u>.

Psa. 139:8

If I <u>ascend to heaven</u>, you are there! If I make my <u>bed in
Sheol</u>, you are there!

Isa. 7:11

"Ask a sign of the LORD your God; let it be <u>deep as Sheol</u>
or <u>high as heaven</u>."

These are not mere references to the body in the grave, but to locations of
the spiritual soul as well. Sheol is a combined term that describes both the grave
for the body and the underworld location of the departed souls of the dead.

In the New Testament, the word *Hades* is used for the underworld,
which was the Greek equivalent of Sheol.[27] Jesus Himself used the term
Hades as the location of damned spirits in contrast with heaven as the
location of redeemed spirits when He talked of Capernaum rejecting
miracles, "And you, Capernaum, will you be <u>exalted to heaven</u>? You will be
<u>brought down to Hades</u> (Matt. 11:23)." Hades was also the location of
departed spirits in His parable of Lazarus and the rich man in Hades (Luke
16:19-31).

---

[27] "Hades," *DDD*, p 382.

In Greek mythology, Tartarus was another term for a location beneath the "roots of the earth" and beneath the waters where the warring giants called "Titans" were bound in chains because of their rebellion against the gods.[28] Peter uses a derivative of that very Greek word Tartarus to describe a similar location and scenario of angels being bound during the time of Noah and the warring Titans called "Nephilim."[29]

2 Pet. 2:4-5

For if God did not spare <u>angels</u> when they sinned, but <u>cast them into hell [*tartaroo*] and committed them to chains</u> of gloomy darkness to be kept until the judgment; if He did not spare the ancient world, but preserved Noah.

The Watery Abyss

In Mesopotamian cosmography, the Abyss (*Apsu* in Akkadian) was a cosmic subterranean lake or body of water that was between the earth and the underworld (Sheol), and was the source of the waters above such as oceans, rivers, and springs or fountains.[30] In *The Epic of Gilgamesh*, Utnapishtim, the Babylonian Noah, tells his fellow citizens that he is building his boat and will abandon the earth of Enlil to join Ea in the waters of the Abyss that would soon fill the land.[31] Even bitumen pools used to

---

[28] "They then conducted them [the Titans] under the highways of the earth as far below the ground as the ground is below the sky, and tied them with cruel chains. So far down below the ground is gloomy Tartarus...Tartarus is surrounded by a bronze moat...above which the roots of earth and barren sea are planted. In that gloomy underground region the Titans were imprisoned by the decree of Zeus." Norman Brown, Trans. *Theogony: Hesiod.* New York: Bobbs-Merrill Co., 1953, p 73-4.

[29] 1.25 ταρταρόω [*tartaroo*] Louw, Johannes P., and Eugene Albert Nida. *Greek-English Lexicon of the New Testament : Based on Semantic Domains.* electronic ed. of the 2nd edition. New York: United Bible societies, 1996. Bauckham, Richard J. Vol. 50, *Word Biblical Commentary : 2 Peter, Jude.* Word Biblical Commentary. Dallas: Word, Incorporated, 2002, p 248-249.

[30] Horowitz, *Mesopotamian Cosmic Geography*, p 334-348.

[31] *The Epic of Gilgamesh* XI:40-44. *The Ancient Near East an Anthology of Texts and Pictures.* Edited by James Bennett Pritchard. Princeton: Princeton University Press, 1958, p 93.

make pitch were thought to rise up from the "underground waters," or the Abyss.[32]

Similarly, in the Bible the earth also rests on the seas or "the deep" (*tehom*) that produces the springs and waters from its subterranean waters below the earth.

> Psa. 24:1-2
> The world, and those who dwell therein, for He has <u>founded</u> <u>it upon the seas,</u> and established it upon the rivers.

> Psa. 136:6
> To Him who spread out the earth <u>above the waters.</u>

> Gen. 49: 25
> The Almighty who will bless you with blessings of heaven above, Blessings of <u>the deep that crouches beneath.</u>

> Exod. 20:4
> You shall not make for yourself a carved image, or any likeness of anything that is in heaven above, or that is in the earth beneath, or that is <u>in the water under the earth.</u>

Leviathan is even said to dwell in the Abyss in Job 41:24 (LXX)[33]. When God brings the flood, part of the waters are from "the fountains of the great deep" bursting open (Gen. 7:11; 8:2).

The Firmament

If we move upward in the registers of cosmography, we find another ancient paradigm of the heavens covering the earth like a solid dome or vault with the sun, moon, and stars embedded in the firmament yet still somehow

---

[32] Horowitz, *Mesopotamian Cosmic Geography*, p 337.
[33] "[Leviathan] regards the netherworld [Tartauros] of the deep [Abyss] like a prisoner. He regards the deep [Abyss] as a walk." Job 41:34, Tan, Randall, David A. deSilva, and Logos Bible Software. *The Lexham Greek-English Interlinear Septuagint.* Logos Bible Software, 2009.

able to go around the earth. Reformed scholar Paul Seely has done key research on this notion.[34]

> Gen. 1:6-8
> And God said, "Let there be an <u>expanse</u> [firmament] in the midst of the waters, and let it separate the waters from the waters." And God made the <u>expanse</u> [firmament] and separated the waters that were under the <u>expanse</u> [firmament] from the waters that were above the <u>expanse</u> [firmament]. And it was so. And God called the <u>expanse</u> [firmament] Heaven.

I used to think, what is that all about? Waters below separated from waters above by the sky? Some try to explain those waters above as a water canopy above the earth that came down at Noah's flood. But that doesn't make sense Biblically because birds are said to "fly over the <u>face</u> of the firmament" (Gen. 1:20) with the same Hebrew grammar as God's Spirit hovering "over the <u>face</u> of the waters" (Gen. 1:2). The firmament cannot be the "water canopy" because the firmament is not the waters, *but the object that is separating and holding back the waters*. If the firmament is an "expanse" or the sky itself, then the birds would be flying *within* the firmament, not *over the face of* the firmament as the text states. So the firmament cannot be a water canopy and it cannot be the sky itself.

The T.K.O. of the canopy theory is the fact that according to the Bible those "waters above" and the firmament that holds them back were still considered in place during the time of King David long after the flood:

> Psa. 104:2-3
> Stretching out the heavens like a tent. He lays the beams of His chambers on the waters;

---

[34] "The Firmament And The Water Above: Part I: The Meaning Of Raqia In Gen 1:6-8," Paul H. Seely, *The Westminster Theological Journal* 53 (1991) 227-40. http://faculty.gordon.edu/hu/bi/ted_hildebrandt/OTeSources/01-Genesis/Text/Articles-Books/Seely-Firmament-WTJ.pdf

Psa. 148:4

Praise Him, you highest heavens, and you waters above the heavens!

Seely shows how modern scientific bias has guided the translators to render the word for "firmament" (*raqia*) as "expanse." *Raqia* in the Bible consistently means a solid material such as a metal that is hammered out by a craftsman (Exod. 39:3; Isa. 40:19). And when *raqia* is used elsewhere in the Bible for the heavens, it clearly refers to a solid crystalline material, sometimes even metal!

Job 37:18

Can you, like Him, spread out [*raqia*] the skies, hard as a cast metal mirror?

Exod. 24:10

And they saw the God of Israel. There was under His feet as it were a pavement [*raqia*] of sapphire stone, like the very heaven for clearness.

Ezek. 1:22-23

Over the heads of the living creatures there was the likeness of an expanse [*raqia*], shining like awe-inspiring crystal, spread out above their heads. And under the expanse [*raqia*] their wings were stretched out straight.

Prov. 8:27-28

When He established the heavens... when He made firm the skies above.

Job 22:14

He walks on the vault of heaven.

Amos 9:6
[God] builds His upper chambers in the heavens and founds
His vault upon the earth.

Not only did the ancient translators of the Septuagint (LXX) translate *raqia* into the Latin equivalent for a hard firm solid surface (*firmamentum*), but also the Jews of the Second Temple period consistently understood the word *raqia* to mean a solid surface that covered the earth like a dome. Consider these examples of 2nd Temple literature:

3 Bar. 3:6-8
And the Lord appeared to them and confused their speech, when they had built the tower... And they took a gimlet, and sought to <u>pierce the heaven</u>, saying, <u>Let us see (whether) the heaven is made of clay, or of brass, or of iron.</u>

2 Apoc. Bar. 21:4
'O you that have made the earth, hear me, that have <u>fixed the firmament</u> by the word, and have <u>made firm the height of the heaven.</u>

Josephus, *Antiquities* 1:30 (1.1.1.30)
On the second day, he placed the heaven over the whole world... He also placed <u>a crystalline [firmament] round it.</u>

The Talmud describes rabbis debating over which remains fixed and which revolves, the constellations or the solid sky (Pesachim 94b),[35] as well as how to calculate the thickness of the firmament scientifically (Pesab. 49a) and Biblically (Genesis Rabbah 4.5.2).[36] While the Talmud is not the definitive interpretation of the Bible, it certainly illustrates how ancient Jews of that time period understood the term, which can be helpful in learning the Hebrew cultural context.

---

[35] Quoted in The Science in Torah: the Scientific Knowledge of the Talmudic Sages By Leo Levi, page 90-91.
[36] Seely, "The Firmament," p 236.

When the Scriptures talk poetically of this vault of heaven it uses the same terminology of stretching out the solid surface of the heavens over the earth *as it does of stretching out an ancient desert tent over the flat ground* (Isa. 54:2; Jer. 10:20) — not like an expanding Einsteinian time-space atmosphere.

> Psa. 19:4
> He has set a tent for the sun.

> Psa. 104:2
> Stretching out the heavens like a tent.

> Isa. 45:12
> It was my hands that stretched out the heavens,

> Isa. 51:13
> The LORD... who stretched out the heavens and laid the foundations of the earth.

> Jer. 10:12
> It is He who established the world by His wisdom, and by His understanding stretched out the heavens.

> Jer. 51:15
> It is He who established the world by His wisdom, and by His understanding stretched out the heavens.

Keeping this tent-like vault over the earth in mind, when God prophesies about the physical destruction He will bring upon a nation, He uses the symbolism of rolling up that firmament like the tent He originally stretched out (or a scroll), along with the shaking of the pillars of the earth and the pillars of heaven which results in the stars falling from the heavens because they were embedded within it.

Isa. 34:4

All the host of heaven shall rot away, and the skies roll up like a scroll. All their host shall fall, as leaves fall from the vine.

Rev. 6:13-14

[An earthquake occurs] and the stars of the sky fell to the earth as the fig tree sheds its winter fruit when shaken by a gale. The sky vanished like a scroll that is being rolled up, and every mountain and island was removed from its place.

Matt. 24:29

"The stars will fall from heaven, and the powers of the heavens will be shaken."

Job 26:11

"The pillars of heaven tremble, and are astounded at His rebuke.

2 Sam. 22:8

Then the earth reeled and rocked; the foundations of the heavens trembled and quaked.

Isa. 13:13

Therefore I shall make the heavens tremble, and the earth will be shaken out of its place at the wrath of the LORD of hosts.

Joel 2:10

The earth quakes before them, the heavens tremble.

Waters Above the Heavens

Now on to the highest point of the Mesopotamian cosmography, the "highest heavens," or "heaven of heavens," where God has established His temple and throne (Deut. 26:15; Psa. 11:4; 33:13; 103:19). But God's throne also happens to be in the midst of a sea of waters that reside there. These are the waters that are above the firmament, that the firmament holds back from falling to earth (Gen. 1:6-8).

Psa. 148:4
Praise Him, you highest heavens, and you <u>waters above the heavens</u>!

Psa. 104:2-3
Stretching out the heavens like a tent. He lays the <u>beams of His chambers on the waters</u>.

Psa. 29:3, 10
The voice of the <u>LORD is over the waters</u>... the LORD, <u>over many waters</u>... The LORD sits <u>enthroned over the flood</u> [not a reference to the flood of Noah, but to these floodwaters above the heavens][37] the LORD sits enthroned as king forever.

Jer. 10:13
When He utters His voice, there is a tumult of <u>waters in the heavens,</u>

Ezek. 28:2
"I sit in the seat of the gods, in the heart of the seas."

The solid firmament that holds back the heavenly waters has "windows of the heavens" ("floodgates" in the NASB) that let the water through to flood the earth in Noah's day.

---

[37] Robert G. Bratcher, and William David Reyburn. *A Translator's Handbook on the Book of Psalms.* Helps for translators. New York: United Bible Societies, 1991, p 280. Psalm 29 takes place in heaven amidst God's heavenly host around his throne.

Gen. 7:11
All the fountains of the great deep burst forth, and the windows of the heavens were opened.

Gen. 8:2
The fountains of the deep and the windows of the heavens were closed, and the rain from the heavens was restrained.

Isa. 24:18
For the windows of heaven are opened, and the foundations of the earth tremble.

Summary of Mesopotamian Cosmography in Scriptures

The sheer volume of passages throughout both Testaments illustrating the parallels with Mesopotamian cosmography seems to prove a deeply rooted ancient pre-scientific worldview that permeates the Scriptures, and this worldview is not coincident with modern science. Here is a summary listing of its elements (extra-biblical 2nd Temple literature in parentheses):

Three-Tiered Universe
Gen. 28:12, 17; Exod. 20:4; Rev. 5:3, 13; Phil. 2:10; Luke 16:19-31; (2 Esdr. 4:7).

God's Throne on Waters Above the Heavens
Gen. 7:11; 8:2; Deut. 26:15; Psa. 11:4; 33:13; 103:19; 104:2; 29:3, 10; 104:2-3; 148:4; Jer. 10:12-13; Ezek 28:2; (2 Esdr. 4:7-8).

Floodgates in the Heavens
Gen. 7:11; 8:2; Isa. 24:11.

Solid Firmament Vault over the Earth
Gen. 1:6-8, 20; Job 37:18; Exod. 24:10; Job 22:14; Ezek. 1:22-26; Psa. 19:4-6; 104:2; Isa. 40:22; Prov. 8:27-28; Isa.

45:12; 51:13-14; Jer. 10:12; 51:15; Isa. 34:4; Amos 9:7; Rev. 6:13-14; (3 Baruch 3:6-8; 2 Apoc. Baruch 21:4; 2 Enoch 3:3; Pesachim 94b; Peab. 49a; Gen. Rabbah 4.5.2; Josephus *Antiquities* 1:30).

Stars Embedded in the Firmament
Matt. 24:29; Isa. 34:4; Rev. 6:13; Dan. 8:10; (Sibyl. 5:514).

Flat Disc Earth Surrounded by Circumferential Sea
Prov. 8:27-29; Job 26:10-11; Psa. 19:6; 72:8; Zech. 9:10; Isa. 40:22; Rev. 7:1; 20:8; Isa. 11:12; Ezek. 7:2; Dan. 4:10-11, 32-33; Matt. 4:8; Isa. 13:5; 41:8-9; Matt. 12:42; Job 37:3; Matt. 24:31; Job 38:12-13; Psa. 136:6; Isa. 42:4; 44:24; Job 11:9; 38:18.

Geocentricity
Psa. 19:4-6; 50:1; Eccl. 1:5; Josh. 10:13; Matt. 5:45.

Immovable Earth
1 Chr. 16:30; Psa. 75:3; 93:1; 96:10; 104:5.

Pillars under the Earth
Psa. 75:3; 104:5; Job 38:4-6; 26:6; 1 Sam. 2:8; 22:16; Zech. 12:1; Prov. 8:29; (Targum Job 26:7).

Pillars under the Heavens
Job 26:11; 2 Sam. 22:8; Isa. 13:13; Joel 2:10.

Watery Abyss Below the Earth
Gen. 49:25; Psa. 24:1-2; 136:6; Dan. 33:13.

Sheol Below the Earth
Num. 16:31-33; 1 Sam. 28:13-15; Isa. 14:9-11; Amos 9:2; Matt. 1:23; Luke 10:15; 16:23; Rev. 20:14; 2 Pet. 2:4-5 (with 1 Pet. 3:18-20).

So, What's Wrong With the Bible?

The cosmic geography of the ancient Near East as revealed in Scripture consists of a three-tiered universe with God on a heavenly throne above a heavenly sea, underneath which is a solid vaulted dome with the sun, moon, and stars connected to it, covering the flat disc earth, founded immovably firm on pillars, surrounded by a circular sea, on top of a watery abyss, beneath which is the underworld of Sheol.

Some well-intentioned Evangelicals seek to maintain their particular definition of Biblical inerrancy by denying that the Bible contains this ancient Near Eastern cosmography. They try to explain it away as phenomenal language or poetic license. Phenomenal language is the act of describing what one sees subjectively from one's perspective without further claiming objective reality. So when the writer says the sun stood still, or that the sun rises and sets within the solid dome of heaven, he is only describing his observation, not cosmic reality. The claim of observation from a personal frame of reference is certainly true as far as it goes. Of course the observer describes what they are observing. But the distinction between appearance and reality is an imposition of our alien modern understanding onto theirs. As Seely explains,

> It is precisely because ancient peoples were scientifically naive that they did not distinguish between the appearance of the sky and their scientific concept of the sky. They had no reason to doubt what their eyes told them was true, namely, that the stars above them were fixed in a solid dome and that the sky literally touched the earth at the horizon. So, they equated appearance with reality and concluded that the sky must be a solid physical part of the universe just as much as the earth itself.[38]

If the ancients did not know the earth was a sphere in space, they could not know that their observations of a flat earth were anything other than what

---

[38] Seely, "The Firmament," p 228.

they observed. It would be easy enough to relegate one or two examples of Scripture to the notion of phenomenal language, but when dozens of those phenomenal descriptions reflect the same complex integrated picture of the universe that Israel's neighbors shared, and when that picture included many elements that were *not* phenomenally observable, such as the Abyss, Sheol, or the pillars of earth and heaven, it strains credulity to suggest these were merely phenomenal descriptions intentionally unrelated to reality. If it walks like an ancient Near Eastern duck and talks like an ancient Near Eastern duck, then chances are they thought it was an ancient Near Eastern duck, not just the "appearance" of one having no reality.

It would also be a mistake to claim that there is a single monolithic Mesopotamian cosmography.[39] There are varieties of stories with overlapping imagery, and some contradictory notions. But there are certainly enough commonalities to affirm a generic yet mysterious picture of the universe. And that picture in Scripture undeniably includes poetic language. The Hebrew culture was imaginative. They integrated poetry into everything, including their observational descriptions of nature. Thus a hymn of creation such as Psalm 19 tells of the heavens declaring God's glory as if using speech, and then describes the operations of the sun in terms of a bridegroom in his chamber or a man running a race. Metaphor is inescapable and ubiquitous.

And herein lies a potential solution for the dilemma of the scientific inaccuracy of the Mesopotamian cosmic geography in Scripture: *The Israelite culture, being pre-scientific, thought more in terms of function and purpose than material structure.* Even if their picture of the heavens and earth as a three-tiered geocentric cosmology, was scientifically "false," from our modern perspective, it nevertheless still accurately describes the teleological purpose and meaning of creation that they were intending to communicate.

Othmar Keel, one of the leading scholars on Ancient Near Eastern art has argued that even though modern depictions of the ancient worldview like the illustration of the three-tiered universe above are helpful, they are

---

[39] Horowitz, *Mesopotamian Cosmic Geography.*

fundamentally flawed because they depict a "profane, lifeless, virtually closed mechanical system," which reflects our own modern bias. To the ancient Near East "rather, the world was an entity open at every side. The powers which determine the world are of more interest to the ancient Near East than the structure of the cosmic system. A wide variety of diverse, uncoordinated notions regarding the cosmic structure were advanced from various points of departure."[40]

John Walton has written recently of this ANE concern with powers over structure in direct relation to the creation story of Genesis. He argues that in the ancient world existence was understood more in terms of function within a god-created *purposeful order* than in terms of material status within a natural physical structure.[41] This is not to say that the physical world was denied or ignored, but rather that the priority and interests were different from our own. We should therefore be careful in judging their purpose-driven cosmography too strictly in light of our own material-driven cosmography. And in this sense, modern material descriptions of reality are just as "false" as the ancient pictures because they do not include the immaterial aspect of reality: Meaning and purpose.

Biblical writers did not *teach* their cosmography as scientific doctrine revealed by God about the way the physical universe was materially structured, they *assumed* the popular cosmography to teach their doctrine about God's purposes and intent. To critique the cosmic model carrying the message is to miss the meaning altogether, which is the message. God's throne may not be physically above us in waters held back by a solid firmament, but He truly does rule "over" us and is king and sustainer of creation in whatever model man uses to depict that creation. The phrase "every created thing which is in heaven and on the earth and under the earth" (Rev. 5:13) is equivalent in meaning to the modern concept of every particle and wave in every dimension of the Big Bang space-time continuum, as well as every person dead or alive in heaven or hell.

The geocentric picture in Scripture is a depiction through man's ancient perspective of God's purpose and humankind's significance. For a modern

---

[40] Othmar Keel, *The Symbolism of the Biblical World*, Winona Lake; IN: Eisenbrauns, 1972, 1997, 56-57.
[41] John H. Walton, *The Lost World of Genesis One: Ancient Cosmology and the Origins Debate* (Downers Grove: IL, InterVarsity Press, 2009), 23-36.

heliocentrist to attack that picture as falsifying the theology would be cultural imperialism of the worst kind. Reducing significance to physical location is simply a prejudice of material priority over spiritual purpose.

One of the humorous ironies of this debate is that if the history of science is any judge, a thousand years from now, scientists will no doubt consider our current paradigm with which we judge the ancients to be itself fatally flawed. This is not to reduce reality to relativism, but rather to illustrate that all claims of empirical knowledge contain an inescapable element of human fallibility and finitude. A well-meaning "concordist" Christian who believes that the Bible was revealing scientific truths before their time must ask themselves just which "scientific truths" do they think it is, the Ptolemaic universe that Christians believed before Galileo, the Newtonian clockwork universe that Christians believed in the 17th century, the Einsteinian relative universe that Christians believe in the present, or the future unknown picture of the universe yet to be posited? As soon as they tie their faith to one paradigm, when that paradigm is overthrown they will have to change their interpretation again, or give up their Faith. Scientific paradigms by definition are man-centered because they describe our finite perceptions, not necessarily ultimate reality. A proper response should be a bit more humility and a bit less hubris regarding the use of our own scientific models as standards in judging theological meaning or purpose.

On the other hand, the skeptic who says that the Bible is scientifically false and therefore unreliable myth reducible to mere human construction assumes the same criteria of judgment as the Evangelical Christian who says that the Bible must be scientifically accurate or it is not the Word of God. They both assume the fallacy that precision of physical description verifies the accuracy of transcendent meaning or interpretation. The worldview that most accurately depicts material structure is the one that knows true meaning. The proposition that a scientifically "false" description can communicate spiritual truth or meaning becomes an outrageous truth claim. But is it really so outrageous?

If a young child asks where babies come from, who is right: The father who says, "from mommy's tummy," the scientist who says, "no, from your mother and father," or the pastor who says, "from God."[42] Answer: They are all right and all wrong, depending on the frame of reference (my Einstein bias). The father is scientifically imprecise in his structural definition. The baby actually comes from the uterus. But for a young child, the father must alter his language to accommodate the child's own context and understanding or the child will simply not understand. But the truth claim is still true enough despite the lack of scientific precision. Though the scientist is more precise, he too must adapt his description to the child and suffers the falsity of attributing creative powers to the humans whose genetics are not determined by their choices. Lastly, the pastor is imprecise in that the baby does not come *directly* from God to the world, as his statement may imply, but is mediated through human behavior and genetics. But he is right in that ultimately, God is the origin of all created things and certainly in terms of meaning, God gives that baby its meaning of existence.

Knowledge of the material world is simply not the only form of legitimate knowledge. So now, imagine the foolishness of that scientist spending his time and energy trying to discredit loving fathers and pastors for using imprecise descriptions of biology in their answer to the child. As the child grows into a young adult, she will become more precise or accurate in her understanding of just exactly where babies come from in a scientific sense, but that knowledge has no bearing on the enduring truth that babies come from mommy's tummy and from God. God remains the transcendent origin of that baby as well as its provider of significance and meaning, something science simply cannot discover in material processes alone.

So, now our modern cosmography/cosmology is more precise than the Mesopotamian cosmography assumed by the Biblical writers, but that does not discredit the intent of the Scriptural picture which is to give glory to God for His sovereign origin and control of creation. Even in today's modern world I can still affirm with full truthfulness that...

Psa. 19:1-6
The heavens declare the glory of God,
and the sky above proclaims His handiwork.

Day to day pours out speech,
and night to night reveals knowledge.
There is no speech, nor are there words,
whose voice is not heard.
Their voice goes out through all the earth,
and their words to the end of the world.
In them He has set a tent for the sun,
which comes out like a bridegroom leaving his chamber,
and, like a strong man, runs its course with joy.
Its rising is from the end of the heavens,
and its circuit to the end of them,
and there is nothing hidden from its heat.

Rev. 5:13
And every created thing which is in heaven and on the earth
and under the earth and on the sea, and all things in them, I
heard saying, "To Him who sits on the throne, and to the
Lamb, be blessing and honor and glory and dominion
forever and ever."

CHAPTER 5

New Testament Storytelling Apologetics

This chapter has been adapted from the article, "Storytelling as Subversive Apologetics: A New View from the Hill in Acts 17" in the Christian Research Journal Vol. 30 / No. 02 / 2007.

In Acts 17:16–34, the apostle Paul presents and defends the Gospel to the pagans of his day at the Areopagus in Athens. The Areopagus (from the Greek *Areios pagos*, meaning "Hill of Ares") was named after the Greek god Ares; when the Roman god Mars was linked with Ares, the spot also became known as Mars' Hill.[1] Athens, especially this hill, was the primary location where the Greek and Roman poets, the cultural leaders of the ancient world, met to exchange ideas (v. 21). The poets would espouse philosophy through didactical tracts, oration, and poems and plays for the populace, just as the popular artists of today propagate pagan worldviews through music, television, and feature films from the Hollywood hill.

Paul's Areopagus discourse has been used to justify opposing theories of apologetics by Christian cross-cultural evangelists, theologians, and apologists alike. It has been interpreted as being a Hellenistic (i.e., culturally Greek) sermon (Martin Dibelius) as well as being entirely antithetical to Hellenism (Cornelius Van Til, F. F. Bruce). Dibelius concludes, "The point at issue is whether it is the Old Testament view of history or the philosophical — particularly the Stoic — view of the world that prevails in the speech on the Areopagus. The difference of opinion that we find among the commentators seems to offer little prospect of a definite solution."[2]

---

[1] See *Wikipedia, the Free Encyclopedia,* s.v. "Areopagus," the Wikimedia Foundation, Inc., http://en.wikipedia.org/wiki/Areopagus. See also *The Columbia Encyclopedia*, 6th ed. (New York: Columbia University Press, 2001–05), s. vv. "Mars, in Roman Religion and Mythology," "Mars' Hill," http://www.bartleby.com/65/ma/Mars-god.html, and http://www.bartleby.com/65/ma/MarsHill.html.

[2] Martin Dibelius and K. C. Hanson, *The Book of Acts: Form, Style, and Theology* (Minneapolis: Augsburg Fortress Publishers, 2004), 98.

One thing most differing viewpoints have in common is their emphasis on Paul's discourse as rational debate or empirical proof. What they all seem to miss is the narrative structure of his presentation. Perhaps it is this narrative structure that contains the solution to Dibelius' dilemma. An examination of that structure reveals that Paul does not so much engage in dialectic as he does *retell the pagan story* within a Christian framework.

First, our examination must put Paul's presentation in context. He is brought to the Areopagus, which was not merely the name of a location, but also the name of the administrative and judicial body that met there, the highest court in Athens. The Areopagus formally examined and charged violators of the Roman law against "illicit" new religions.[3] Though the context suggests an open public interaction and not a formal trial, Luke, the narrator, attempts to cast Paul in Athenian narrative metaphor to Socrates, someone with whom the Athenians would be both familiar and uncomfortable. It was Socrates who Xenophon said was condemned and executed for being "guilty of rejecting the gods acknowledged by the state and of bringing in new divinities."[4] Luke uses a similar phrase to describe Paul when he conveys the accusation from some of the philosophers against Paul in verse 18: "He seems to be a proclaimer of strange deities."[5] Luke depicts Paul from the start as a heroically defiant Socrates, a philosopher of truth against the mob.

Exploring Paul's Story

Paul's sermon clearly contains Biblical truths that are found in both Old and New Testaments: God as transcendent creator and sustainer, His providential control of reality, Christ's resurrection, and the final judgment. It is highly significant to note, however, that throughout the entire discourse Paul did not quote a single Scripture to these unbelievers. Paul certainly was not ashamed of the Gospel and regularly quoted Scriptural references when he considered it appropriate (Acts 17:13; 21:17–21; 23:5; 26:22–23; 28:23–28); therefore, his avoidance of Scripture in this instance is instructive of

---

[3] Robert L. Gallagher and Paul Hertig, *Mission in Acts: Ancient Narratives in Contemporary Context* (Maryknoll, NY: Orbis Books, 2004), 224–25.
[4] Xenophon, *Memorabilia*, chap. 1. See also Plato, *Apology* 24B-C; *Euthyphro* 1C; 2B; 3B.
[5] All Scripture quotations are from the New American Standard Bible.

how to preach and defend the gospel to pagans. Quoting chapter and verse may work with those who are already disposed toward God or the Bible, but Paul appears to consider it inappropriate to do so with those who are hostile or opposed to the faith. Witherington adds, "Arguments are only persuasive if they work within the plausibility structure existing in the minds of the hearers."[6] Paul, rather than quoting the Bible like an alien proof-text of propositional doctrines, addresses them using the narrative of the Stoic worldview.

Stoic Narrative

Missions scholars Robert Gallagher and Paul Hertig explain that the facts of Paul's speech mimic the major points of Stoic beliefs. They quote the ancient Roman academic Cicero who outlines these Stoic beliefs: "First, they prove that gods exist; next they explain their nature; then they show that the world is governed by them; and lastly that they care for the fortunes of mankind."[7] The correspondence of these themes with what Paul has to say about God shows that he approaches this topic in the standard way that would have been expected by his audience. He thus establishes his credibility as one who should claim their attention.

Paul enters into the discourse of his listeners; he plays according to the rules of the community he is trying to reach. An examination of each point he makes in his oration will reveal that the identification he is making with their culture is not merely with their structural procedures of argument, but with the narrative of the Stoic worldview. He is retelling the Stoic story through a Christian metanarrative.[8]

Verse 22

"Men of Athens, I observe that you are very religious in all respects."

---

[6] Ben Witherington III, *The Acts of the Apostles: A Socio-Rhetorical Commentary* (Grand Rapids: Eerdmans, 1998), 530.

[7] Cicero, *On The Nature of the Gods* 2.4, quoted in Gallagher and Hertig, 230.

[8] Although the text reveals that both Epicureans and Stoics were there (Acts 17:17–18), it appears that Paul chooses Stoicism to identify with, perhaps because of its closer affinity with the elements of his intended message.

Paul begins his address with the Athenian rhetorical convention, "Men of Athens," noted by such luminary Greeks as Aristotle and Demosthenes.[9] He then affirms their religiosity, which also had been acknowledged by the famous Athenian dramatist Sophocles: "Athens is held of states, the most devout"; and the Greek geographer Pausanias: "Athenians more than others venerate the gods."[10]

Verse 23

"I also found an altar with this inscription, 'TO AN UNKNOWN GOD.' Therefore what you worship in ignorance, this I proclaim to you."

This "Unknown God" inscription may have been the Athenian attempt to hedge their bets against any god they may have missed paying homage to out of ignorance.[11] Paul quoted the ambiguous text as a point of departure for reflections on true worship, which was the same conventional technique Pseudo-Heraclitus used in his *Fourth Epistle*.[12]

Verse 24

"The God who made the world and all things in it, since He is Lord of heaven and earth, does not dwell in temples made with hands."

The Greeks had many sacred temples throughout the ancient world as houses for their gods. The Stoics and other cultural critics, however, considered such attempts at housing the transcendent incorporeal nature of deity to be laughable. Zeno, the founder of Stoicism, was known to have

---

[9] Aristotle, *Pan. Or.* 1, Demosthenes, *Exordia* 54, quoted in Witherington, 520.
[10] Sophocles, *Oedipus Tyrannus*, 260; Pausanias, *Description of Greece*, 1.17.1, quoted in Charles H. Talbert, *Reading Acts: A Literary and Theological Commentary on the Acts of the Apostles* (Macon, GA: Smyth and Helwys Publishing, 2001), 153.
[11] Dibelius and Hanson, 103.
[12] Talbert, 153.

taught that "temples are not to be built to the gods."[13] Euripides, the celebrated Athenian tragedian, foreshadowed Paul's own words with the rhetorical question, "What house fashioned by builders could contain the divine form within enclosed walls?"[14] The Hebrew tradition also carried such repudiation of a physical dwelling place for God (1 Kgs. 8:27) but the context of Paul's speech rings particularly sympathetic to the Stoics residing in the midst of the sacred hill of the Athenian Acropolis, populated by a multitude of temples such as the Parthenon, the Erechtheion, the Temple of Nike, and the Athenia Polias.

Verse 25

"Nor is He served by human hands, as though He needed anything, since He Himself gives to all people life and breath and all things,"

The idea that God does not need humankind, but that humankind needs God as its creator and sustainer is common enough in Hebrew thought (Psa. 50:9–12), but as Dibelius points out:

> The use of the word "serve" is, however, almost unknown in the Greek translation of the Bible, but quite familiar in original Greek (pagan) texts, and in the context with which we are acquainted. The deity is too great to need my "service," we read in the famous chapter of Xenophon's *Memorabilia*, which contains the teleological proof of God.[15]

Seneca wrote, "God seeks no servants; He Himself serves mankind," which is also reflected in Euripides' claim that "God has need of nothing."[16] Paul is striking a familiar chord with the Athenian and Stoic narratives.

---

[13] Explained of Zeno by Plutarch in his *Moralia*, 1034B, quoted in Juhana Torkki, "The Dramatic Account of Paul's Encounter with Philosophy: An Analysis of Acts 17:16–34 with Regard to Contemporary Philosophical Debates" (academic dissertation, Helsinki: Helsinki University Printing House, 2004), 105.

[14] Euripides, frag. 968, quoted in F. F. Bruce, *Paul, Apostle of the Heart Set Free* (Cumbria, UK: Paternoster Press Ltd., 2000), 240.

[15] Dibelius and Hanson, 105–6.

[16] Seneca, *Epistle* 95.47; Euripides, *Hercules* 1345–46, quoted in Talbert, 155.

Verse 26a

"and He made from one every nation of mankind,"

Cicero noted that the "universal brotherhood of mankind"[17] was a common theme in Stoicism — although when Stoics spoke of "man" they tended to exclude the barbarians surrounding them.[18] Nevertheless, as Seneca observed, "Nature produced us related to one another, since she created us from the same source and to the same end."[19]

What is striking in Paul's dialogue is that he neglects to mention Adam as the "one" from which we are created, something he readily did when writing to the Romans (Rom. 5:12–21). The Athenians would certainly not be thinking of the Hebrew Adam when they heard that reference to "one." The "one" they would be thinking of would be the gods themselves. Seneca wrote, "All persons, if they are traced back to their origins, are descendents of the gods," and Dio Chrysostom affirmed, "It is from the gods that the race of men is sprung."[20] Paul may have been deliberately ambiguous by not distinguishing his definition of "one" from theirs, in order to maintain consistency with the Stoic Greek narrative without revealing his hand. He is undermining Stoicism with the Christian worldview, which will be confirmed conclusively in a climactic plot twist at the end of his narrative.

Verse 26b

"to live on all the face of the earth, having determined their appointed times [seasons] and the boundaries of their habitation,"

Christians may read this and immediately consider it an expression of God's providential sovereignty over history, as in Genesis 1, where God determines the times and seasons, or in Deuteronomy 32:8 where He separates the sons of men and establishes their "boundaries." Paul's

---

[17] Cicero, *On Duties*, 3.6.28, quoted in Lee, 88.
[18] Bruce, 241.
[19] Seneca, *Epistle* 95.52, quoted in Michelle V. Lee, *Paul, the Stoics, and the Body of Christ* (Cambridge, UK: Cambridge University Press, 2006), 84.
[20] Seneca, *Epistle* 44.1; Dio Chrysostom, *Oration* 30.26, quoted in Talbert, 156.

Athenian audience, however, would refer to their own intellectual heritage on hearing these words. As Juhana Torkki points out, "The idea of God's kinship to humans is unique in the New Testament writings but common in Stoicism. The Stoic [philosopher] Epictetus devoted a whole essay to the subject."[21] Epictetus writes, "How else could things happen so regularly, by God's command as it were? When he tells plants to bloom, they bloom, when he tells them to bear fruit, they bear it…Is God [Zeus] then, not capable of overseeing everything and being present with everything and maintaining a certain distribution with everything?" [22]

Cicero, in one of his *Tusculan Disputations*, writes that seasons and zones of habitation are evidence of God's existence.[23] Paul continues, with every sentence Luke narrates, to engage Stoic thought by retelling its narrative.

Verse 27

"that they would seek God, if perhaps they might grope for Him and find Him, though He is not far from each one of us;"

This image, as one commentator explains, "carries the sense of 'a blind person or the fumbling of a person in the darkness of night,'" as can be found in the writings of Aristophanes and Plato.[24] Christian apologist Greg Bahnsen suggests that it may even be a Homeric literary allusion to the Cyclops blindly groping for Odysseus and his men.[25] In any case, the image is not a positive one. F. F. Bruce affirms the Hellenistic affinities of this section by quoting the Stoic Dio Chrysostom, "primaeval men are described as 'not settled separately by themselves far away from the divine being or

---

[21] Torkki, 87.

[22] Epictetus *Discourse* 1.14, quoted in A. A. Long, *Epictetus: A Stoic and Socratic Guide to Life* (Oxford, UK: Oxford University Press, 2002), 25–26.

[23] Cicero *Tusculan Disputations* 1.28.68–69, quoted in Talbert, 156.

[24] Aristophanes *Ec.* 315, *Pax* 691; Plato *Phaedo* 99b, quoted in Witherington, 528–29.

[25] Greg Bahnsen, *Always Ready: Directions for Defending the Faith*, ed. Robert Booth (Atlanta: American Vision, 1996), 260–61.

outside him, but...sharing his nature.'"[26] Seneca, true to Stoic form, wrote, "God is near you, He is with you, He is within you."[27]

This idea of humanity blindly groping around for what is, in fact, very near it is also a part of scriptural themes (Deut. 28:29), but with a distinct difference. To the Stoic, God's nearness was a pantheistic nearness. They believed everything was a part of God and God was a part of everything, something Paul would vehemently deny (Rom. 1) but, interestingly enough, does not at this point. He is still maintaining a surface connection with the Stoics by affirming the immanence of God without explicitly qualifying it.

Verse 28

"for in Him we live and move and exist, as even some of your own poets have said, 'For we also are His offspring.'"

Paul thus far implicitly has followed the Stoic narrative without qualifying the differences between it and his full narrative. He would certainly be attacked by modern Christian apologist watchdogs for being heretical since he does not qualify his word usage with endless distinctions from the pagans.

He now, however, becomes more explicit in identifying with these pagans. He favorably quotes some of their own poets to affirm even more identity with them. "In Him we live and move and exist" is a line from Epimenides's well-known *Cretica*:

They fashioned a tomb for thee, 'O holy and high one' But thou art not dead; 'thou livest and abidest for ever', *For in thee we live and move and have our being* (emphasis added).[28]

The second line that Paul quotes, "we also are His offspring," is from Epimenides's fellow-countryman Aratus, in his *Phaenomena*:

---

[26] Dio Chrysostom *Olympic Oration* 12:28, quoted in F. F. Bruce, *The Book of the Acts,* New International Commentary on the New Testament, rev. ed. (Grand Rapids: Eerdmans, 1988), 339.
[27] Seneca *Epistle* 41.1–2, quoted in Talbert, 156.
[28] Bruce, *The Book of the Acts* 338–39.

Let us begin with Zeus, Never, O men, let us leave him
Unmentioned. All the ways are full of Zeus,
And all the market-places of human beings. The sea is full
Of him; so are the harbors. In every way we have all to do
with Zeus, *For we are truly his offspring* (emphasis
added).[29]

Aratus was most likely rephrasing Cleanthe's poem *Hymn to Zeus,*
which not only refers to men as God's children, but to Zeus as the sovereign
controller of all — in whom men live and move:

Almighty Zeus, nature's first Cause, governing all things by
law. It is the right of mortals to address thee, For we *who
live and creep upon the earth are all thy children* (emphasis
added).[30]

These are the same elements of Paul's discourse in Acts 17:24-29.

The Stoics themselves had redefined Zeus to be the impersonal
pantheistic force, also called the "logos," as opposed to a personal deity in
the pantheon of Greek gods. This *logos* was still not anything like the
personal God of the Scriptures. What is disturbing about this section is that
Paul does not qualify the pagan quotations that originally were directed to
Zeus. He doesn't clarify by explaining that Zeus is not the God he is talking
about. He simply quotes these hymns of praise to Zeus as if they are in
agreement with the Christian Gospel. The question arises, why does he not
distinguish his Gospel narrative from theirs?

The answer is found in the idea of subversion. Paul is subverting their
concept of God by using common terms with a different definition that he
does not reveal immediately, but that eventually undermines their entire
narrative. He begins with their conventional understanding of God but steers
them eventually to his own.

---

[29] Ibid.
[30] C. Loring Brace, *Unknown God or Inspiration Among Pre-Christian Races* (1890; repr.,
Whitefish, MT: Kessinger Publishing, 2003), 123.

In quoting pagan references to Zeus, Paul was not affirming paganism but was referencing pagan imagery, poems, and plays to make a point of connection with them as fellow humans. The *imago dei* (image of God) in pagans reflects distorted truth, but a kind of truth nonetheless. Paul then recasts and transforms that connection with pagan immanence in support of Christian immanence through the doctrine of transcendence (17:24, 27), the resurrection, and final judgment (17:30–31), but he saves that twist for the end of his sermon.

Verse 29

"We ought not to think that the Divine Nature is like gold or silver or stone, an image formed by the art and thought of man."

Another belief of Stoicism was that the divine nature that permeated all things was not reducible to mere artifacts of humanity's creation. As Epictetus argued, "You are a 'fragment of God'; you have within you a part of Him... Do you suppose that I am speaking of some external God, made of silver or gold? It is within yourself that you bear Him."[31] Zeno taught, "Men shall neither build temples nor make idols." Dio Chrysostom wrote, "The living can only be represented by something that is living."[32] Once again, Paul is not ignoring the Biblical mocking of "idols of silver and gold" as in Psalm 115:4, but is certainly addressing the issue in a language his hearers would understand, the language of the Stoic narrative.

Verse 30

"Therefore having overlooked the times of ignorance,"

For the Stoics, ignorance was an important doctrine. It represented the loss of knowledge that humanity formerly possessed, knowledge of their pantheistic unity with the *logos*. Dio Chrysostom asks in his *Discourses*, "How, then, could they have remained ignorant and conceived no

---

[31] Epictetus, *Discourses* 2.8.11–12, quoted in Gallagher, 232.
[32] Clement of Alexandria, *Miscellanies* 5.76; Dio Chrysostom, *Oration* 12.83, quoted in Talbert, 156.

inkling...[that] they were filled with the divine nature?"[33] Epictetus echoes the same sentiment in one of his *Discourses*, which is quoted in part above: "You are a 'fragment of God'; you have within you a part of Him. Why then are you ignorant of your own kinship? "[34]

Contrarily, Pauline "ignorance" was a willing, responsible ignorance, a hardness of heart that came from sinful violation of God's commands (Eph. 4:17–19). But, yet again, Paul does not articulate this distinction. He instead makes an ambiguous reference to a generic "ignorance" that the Stoics most naturally would interpret in their own terms. As Talbert describes, "In all of this, he has sought the common ground. There is nothing he has said yet that would appear ridiculous to his philosophic audience."[35]

Verses 30–31

"God is now declaring to men that all people everywhere should repent, because He has fixed a day in which He will judge the world in righteousness through a Man whom He has appointed, having furnished proof to all men by raising Him from the dead."

Here is where the subversion of Paul's storytelling rears its head, like the mind-blowing twist of a movie thriller. Everything is not as it seems. Paul the storyteller gets his pagan audience to nod their heads in agreement, only to be thrown for a loop at the end. Repentance, judgment, and the resurrection, all antithetical to the Stoic narrative, form the conclusion of Paul's narrative.

Witherington concludes of this Areopagus speech, "What has happened is that Greek notions have been taken up and given new meaning by placing them in a Jewish-Christian monotheistic context. Apologetics by means of defense and attack is being done, using Greek thought to make monotheistic points. The call for repentance at the end shows where the argument has

---

[33] Dio Chrysostom, *Discourses* 12.27; cf. 12.12, 16, 21, quoted in Gallagher, 229.
[34] Epictetus, *Discourses* 2.8.11–14, quoted in Gallagher, 229.
[35] Talbert, 156.

been going all along — it is not an exercise in diplomacy or compromise but ultimately a call for conversion."[36]

The Stoics believed in a "great conflagration" of fire where the universe would end in the same kind of fire out of which it was created.[37] This was not the fire of damnation, however, as in Christian doctrine. It was rather the cyclical recurrence of what scientific theorists today would call the "oscillating universe." Everything would collapse into fire, and then be recreated again out of that fire and relive the same cycle and development of history over and over again. Paul's call of final, linear, once-for-all judgment by a single man was certainly one of the factors, then, that caused some of these interested philosophers to scorn him (v. 32).

Note again, however, that even here, Paul never gives the name of Jesus. He alludes to Him and *implies* His identity, which seems to maintain a sense of mystery about the narrative. Modern day evangelists would surely criticize Paul for never naming the name of Jesus. Is that not the power of the Gospel? According to Paul, a mere name was not a magical formula or thermometer of orthodoxy. Did everyone know that he was talking about Jesus? At times, silence can be louder than words, and implication can be more alluring than explication.

The other factor sure to provoke the ire of the cosmopolitan Athenian culture-shapers was the proclamation of the resurrection of Jesus. The poet and dramatist Aeschylus wrote what became a prominent Stoic slogan: "When the dust has soaked up a man's blood, once he is dead there is no resurrection."[38] Paul's explicit reference to the resurrection was certainly a part of the twist he used in his subversive storytelling to get the Athenians to listen to what they otherwise might ignore.

Secular Sources

A couple of important observations are in line regarding Paul's reference to pagan poetry and non-Christian mythology. First, it points out that, as an orthodox Pharisee who stressed the separation of holiness, he did

---

[36] Witherington, 524.
[37] Ibid., 526.
[38] Aeschylus, *Eumenides* 647, quoted in Bruce, *Paul, Apostle of the Heart Set Free*, 247.

not consider it unholy to expose himself to the godless media and art forms (books, plays, and poetry) of his day. He did not merely familiarize himself with them, he *studied* them — well enough to be able to quote them and even utilize their narrative. Paul primarily quoted Scripture in his writings, but he also quoted sinners favorably when appropriate.

Second, this appropriation of pagan cultural images and thought forms by Biblical writers reflects more than a mere quoting of popular sayings or shallow cultural reference. It illustrates a redemptive interaction with those thought forms, a certain amount of involvement in, and affirmation of, the prevailing culture, in service to the Gospel. A simple comparison of Paul's sermon in Acts 17 with Cleanthes's *Hymn to Zeus,* a well-known summary of Stoic doctrine, illustrates an almost point-by-point correspondence of narratives.[39] Paul's preaching in Acts 17 is not a shallow usage of mere phrases, but a deep structural identification with Stoic narrative and images that "align with" the gospel. The list of convergences can be summarized thus:

ACTS 17	STOIC NARRATIVE
v. 24–25	The incorporeal nature of God
v. 25	God's self-sufficiency
v. 26	"Oneness" or brotherhood of mankind
v. 26	Providence over seasons and habitations
v. 27	Humanity's blind groping
v. 27–28	Pantheism /Immanence
v.	Zeus/Logos

---

[39] See Cleanthes, "Hymn to Zeus" (trans. M. A. C. Ellery, 1976), Department of Classics, Monmouth College, http://www.utexas.edu/courses/citylife/readings/cleanthes_hymn.html.

28		
v. 28	Humans as God's offspring	
v. 29	Divine nature, not gold or silver	
v. 23, 30	Wisdom vs. ignorance	
v. 30–31	Justice	

Lastly, this incident is not the only place where subversion occurs in the Bible. *The Dictionary of New Testament Background* cites more than 100 New Testament passages that reflect "Examples of Convergence between Pagan and Early Christian Texts." Citations, images and word pictures are quoted, adapted, or appropriated from such pagans as Aeschylus, Sophocles, Plutarch, Tacitus, Xenophon, Aristotle, Seneca, and other Hellenistic cultural sources. The sheer volume of such Biblical reference suggests an interactive intercourse of Scriptural writings with culture rather than absolute separation or shallow manipulation of that culture.[40]

Subversion Vs. Syncretism

Some Christians may react with fear that this kind of redemptive interaction with culture is syncretism, an attempt to fuse two incompatible systems of thought. Subversion, however, is not syncretism. Subversion is what Paul engaged in.

In subversion, the narrative, images, and symbols of one system are discreetly redefined or altered in the new system. Paul quotes a poem to Zeus, but covertly intends a different deity. He superficially affirms the immanence of the Stoic "Universal Reason" that controls and determines all nature and men, yet he describes this universal all-powerful deity as personal rather than as abstract law. He agrees with the Stoics that men are ignorant

---

[40] J.D. Charles, "Examples of Convergence between Pagan and Early Christian Texts," *The Dictionary of New Testament Background* (InterVarsity Christian Fellowship/USA, 2000). Electronic text hypertexted and prepared by OakTree Software, Inc. Version 1.0.

of God and His justice, but then affirms that God proved that He will judge the world through Christ by raising Christ from the dead — two doctrines the Stoics were vehemently against. He affirms the unity of humanity and the immanence of God in all things, but contradicts Stoic pantheism and redefines that immanence by affirming God's transcendence and the Creator/creature distinction. Paul did not reveal these stark differences between the Gospel and the Stoic narrative until the end of his talk. He was subverting paganism, not syncretizing Christianity with it.

Subversive Story Strategy

By casting his presentation of the Gospel in terms that Stoics could identify with and by undermining their narrative with alterations, Paul is strategically subverting through story. Author Curtis Chang, in his book *Engaging Unbelief*, explains this rhetorical strategy as three-fold: "1. Entering the challenger's story, 2. Retelling the story, 3. Capturing that retold tale with the gospel metanarrative."[41] He explains that the claim that we observe evidence objectively and apply reason neutrally to prove our worldview is an artifact of Enlightenment mythology. The truth is that each epoch of thought in history, whether Medieval, Enlightenment, or Postmodern, is a contest in storytelling. "The one who can tell the best story, in a very real sense, wins the epoch."[42]

Chang affirms the inescapability of story and image through history even in philosophical argumentation: "Strikingly, many of the classic philosophical arguments from different traditions seem to take the form of a story: from Plato's scene of the man bound to the chair in the cave to Hobbes's elaborate drama of the 'state of nature,' to John Rawls's 'choosing game.'"[43] Stories may come in many different genres, but we cannot escape them.

Many Christian apologists and theologians have tended to focus on the doctrinal content of Paul's Areopagus speech at the expense of the narrative

---

[41] Curtis Chang, *Engaging Unbelief: A Captivating Strategy from Augustine to Aquinas* (Downers Grove, IL: InterVarsity Press, 2000), 26.
[42] Ibid, 29.
[43] Ibid, 30.

structure that carries the message. There is certainly more proclamation in this passage than rational argument.

The progression of events from creation to fall to redemption that characterize Paul's narrative reflects the beginning, middle, and end of linear Western storytelling. God is Lord, He created all things and created all people from one (creation), then determined the seasons and boundaries. People then became blind and were found groping in the darkness post-Eden, ignorant of their very identity as His children (fall). Then God raised a man from the dead and will judge the world in the future through that same man. Through repentance, people can escape their ignorance and separation from God (redemption). Creation, fall, redemption; beginning, middle, end; Genesis, Covenant, Eschaton are elements of narrative that communicate worldview.

Does this retelling of stories simply reduce persuasion to a relativistic "stand-off" between opposing stories with no criteria for discerning which is true? Scholar N. T. Wright suggests that the way to handle the clash of competing stories is to tell yet another story, one that encompasses and explains the stories of one's opposition, yet contains an explanation for the anomalies or contradictions within those stories:

> There is no such thing as "neutral" or "objective" proof; only the claim that the story we are now telling about the world as a whole makes more sense, in its outline and detail, than other potential or actual stories that may be on offer. Simplicity of outline, elegance in handling the details within it, the inclusion of all the parts of the story, and the ability of the story to make sense beyond its immediate subject-matter: these are what count.[44]

While a significant number of Christian apologists would consider Wright's claim as neglectful of Paul's appeal to evidence elsewhere (v. 31), it is certainly instructive of the opposite neglect that many have had for the legitimate operations of story or narrative coherence in persuasion.

---

[44] N. T. Wright, *The New Testament and the People of God* (Minneapolis: Augsburg Fortress Press, 1992), 42.

Paul tells the story of mankind in Acts 17, a story that encompasses and includes images and elements of the Stoic story, but solves the problems of that system within a more coherent and meaningful story that conveys Christianity. He studies and engages in the Stoic story, retells that story, and captures it with the gospel metanarrative. Paul subverts Stoic paganism with the Christian worldview.

Samples of Subversion

In the first paragraph of this chapter, I mentioned the entertainment of Hollywood as a strong analogy with the influence of the Greek poets. I would like to conclude with an example of a Hollywood movie that uses subversive storytelling in a way similar to Paul on the Areopagus. *The Exorcism of Emily Rose*, written and directed by Scott Derrickson, uses the power of story to subvert the modernist mindset that believes all spiritual beliefs are superstitious misunderstandings of scientific phenomena. *Emily Rose* is based on an allegedly true story of a Roman Catholic priest on trial for criminal negligence in the death of a college girl named Emily Rose. Emily comes to the priest because she believes she is demon possessed. In the midst of a laborious exorcism ritual, she dies from self-inflicted wounds, and the priest goes to trial. The setting of a court is strikingly reminiscent of Paul's standing in the Areopagus, speaking to the "modernist" lawyers and rhetoricians of his day.

Erin Bruner, a female attorney, defends the priest by seeking to prove the "possibility" of demon possession in court. The prosecutor mocks her through the trial, referring to her spiritual arguments as superstition unworthy of legal procedure in a modern scientific world. He then seeks to prove that Emily had epilepsy, which required drugs, not "voodoo," resulting in the priest's blood guiltiness. The movie presents both sides of the argument in court so equally that legal or rational certainty is impossible. The privilege of seeing Emily's experience of demon possession outside that court of law leaves the viewer with a strong sense that the empirical prejudice of modern science has been undermined. Supernatural evil, and by extension, supernatural good (God) are real. Derrickson uses the story to subvert the stranglehold of modernity on the Western mind, and the inadequacy of rationalism and the scientific method in discovering everything there is to know about truth.

Other examples of subversion in Hollywood movies are: *The Island*, which uses a science-fiction action chase film to subvert the utilitarian murderous ethos of our "pro-choice" culture; *The Wicker Man,* a subversion of Wicca and pagan earth worship; and *Apocalypto*, a subversion of the "noble savage" myth of the indigenous native Americans.

The traditional approach to Christian apologetics is the detailed accumulation of rational arguments and empirical evidence for the existence of God, the reliability of the Bible, and the miraculous resurrection of Jesus Christ. The conventional image of a Christian apologist is one who studies apologetics or philosophy at a university, one who wields logical arguments for the existence of God and manuscript evidence for the reliability of the Bible, or one who engages in debates about evolution or Islam. These remain valid and important endeavors, but in a postmodern world focused on narrative discourse we need also to take a lesson from the apostle Paul and expand our avenues for evangelism and defending the faith. We need more Christian apologists writing revisionist biographies of godless deities such as Darwin, Marx, and Freud; writing for and subverting pagan TV sitcoms; bringing a Christian worldview interpretation to their journalism in secular magazines and news reporting; making horror films that undermine the idol of modernity; writing, singing, and playing subversive industrial music, rock music, and rap music. We need to be actively, sacredly subverting the secular stories of the culture, and restoring their fragmented narratives for Christ. If it was good enough for the apostle Paul on top of Mars' Hill then, it's certainly good enough for those of us in the shade of the Hollywood hills now.

CHAPTER 6

Imagination in Prophecy and Apocalypse

This chapter has been adapted from the article, "The Collapsing Universe in the Bible: Literal Science or Poetic Metaphor?" published at BioLogos Foundation.

Creation and Decreation

Rev. 6:12–14

When he opened the sixth seal, I looked, and behold, there was a great earthquake, and the sun became black as sackcloth, the full moon became like blood, and the stars of the sky fell to the earth as the fig tree sheds its winter fruit when shaken by a gale. The sky vanished like a scroll that is being rolled up, and every mountain and island was removed from its place.

As argued in a previous chapter of this book, the non-concordist view of science and Scripture argues that Biblical texts about creation were never intended to concord with modern scientific theories. Thus, Genesis 1 is not cryptically describing the Big Bang or instant fiat, a young earth or old earth, special creation or evolutionary creation. It is not "literal" language describing the physics of the universe, it is "literary" genre describing God's sovereignty over creation and most likely His covenantal relationship with His people.

But the argument against literalism of language of the creation of the heavens and the earth is also applicable to the language of the destruction of the heavens and the earth, or what the Bible calls, "the last days," "the end of the age," "the end of days," or "the Day of the Lord." Christians often refer to this as "the end times," but the technical theological term is *eschatology*, which means "the study of end things."

Regarding the end times, the modern Evangelical popular imagination has been deeply influenced and at times dominated by a theological construct that is best reflected in the 1970s bestselling *The Late Great Planet Earth* by Hal Lindsey and the newer bestselling fictional phenomenon *Left Behind* by Tim LaHaye and Jerry Jenkins.

This view believes that the Bible foretells an as-yet future scenario on the earth of a rapture of Christians, followed by the rise of an "Anti-Christ," a world dictator who initiates a Great Tribulation on the earth, requires a "Mark of the Beast," and assembles global forces for a battle of Armageddon against Israel, resulting in the Second Coming of Christ who replaces the universe with a new heavens and earth to rule forever. The technical theological term for this view is *futurism*, the belief that prophecies about the end times are yet to be fulfilled in the future.[1]

In this chapter, I will address the hermeneutic or interpretive approach used by this futurist perspective and apply it to the particular aspect of creation language, or in this case, decreation language — the collapsing universe and the destruction of the heavens and the earth.

In short, the language of cosmic catastrophe often interpreted literally as referring to the end of the space-time universe is actually used by Biblical authors to figuratively express the cosmic significance of the covenantal relationship between God and humanity.

The tendency of modern literalism is to interpret descriptions of signs in the heavens and earth as being quite literal events of the heavens and earth shaking, stars falling from the sky, the moon turning blood red, and the sky rolling up like a scroll. The problem with this hermeneutic is that it assumes the priority of modernity over the ancient world. Rather than seeking to understand the origins of symbols and images used by the writers within their ancient context, this literalism often suggests the writer was seeing events that would occur in our modern day but did not understand them, so he used his ancient "primitive" language to describe it.

So for instance when the apostle John saw modern day tools of war in his revelation, such as battle helicopters, he did not know what they were so

---

[1] The *Left Behind* series is a particular version of futurism called Dispensational Premillennialism. For a more in depth presentation of these varieties of eschatology see Bock, Darrell L. ed., *Three Views on the Millennium and Beyond*. Grand Rapids, MI: Zondervan, 1999.

he described them in ancient terms that he did understand such as locusts with the sting of scorpions, breastplates of iron, a crown of gold and human faces, whose chopper blades made the "noise of many chariots with horses rushing into battle" (Rev. 9:3-9).

I was taught this modernist interpretation and lived by it for many years. When I read about Jesus explaining the "end of the age" I would assume He meant the "end of the space-time universe" because that's the kind of language I, a post-Enlightened modern scientific mind, would use to describe such an event. When He spoke of the moon turning blood red and the sun being darkened, I assumed such events were easy miracles for God, so if you considered them figurative, you were falling down the slippery slope of neo-orthodoxy. When Jesus said stars would fall from the sky, you had better bet stars would literally fall from the sky (a primitive description of meteors[2]) or else you're a liberal who doesn't believe in the literal accuracy of the Bible.

But all that changed when I sought to understand the prophetic discourse on its own terms within its ancient cultural context instead of from my own cultural bias. I now propose that the ancient writers did understand what they were seeing, but were using mythopoeic symbols and images they were culturally steeped in, symbols and images with a history of usage from the Old Testament, *their* cultural context — not mine.

In this essay, I will argue that the decreation language of a collapsing universe with falling stars and signs in the heavens was actually symbolic discourse about world-changing events and powers related to the end of the old covenant and the coming of the new covenant as God's "new world order." In this interpretation, predictions of the collapsing universe were figuratively fulfilled in the historic past of the first century. The technical theological term for this view is *preterism*, the belief that prophecies about the end times have been fulfilled in the past.[3]

---

[2] Interestingly, as soon as the interpreter thinks falling stars are meteors, he has just engaged in figurative speculation, which is not literal.

[3] An example of orthodox scholars who hold to this view are Sproul, R.C. *The Last Days According to Jesus.* Grand Rapids, MI: Baker, 1998; and Gentry, Kenneth L. Jr. *Navigating the Book of Revelation.* Fountain Inn: SC, Goodbirth Ministries, 2009.

Sun, Moon and Stars

First, let's take a look at the usage of sun, moon and stars in the Old Testament. In the ancient Near East, there is often a conceptual equivalency or link between stars, heavenly bodies, and deities.[4] The Encyclopedia Judaica notes that, "in many cultures the sky, the sun, the moon, and the known planets were conceived as personal gods. These gods were responsible for all or some aspects of existence. Prayers were addressed to them, offerings were made to them, and their opinions on important matters were sought through divination."[5]

But it was not merely the pagans who made this connection of heavenly physical bodies with heavenly spiritual powers. The Old Testament itself equates the sun, moon, and stars with the angelic "sons of God" who surround God's throne, calling them both the "host of heaven" (Deut. 4:19; 32:8-9).[6] Jewish commentator Jeffrey Tigay writes, "[These passages] seem to reflect a Biblical view that... as punishment for man's repeated spurning of His authority in primordial times (Gen. 3-11), God deprived mankind at large of true knowledge of Himself and ordained that it should worship idols and subordinate celestial beings."[7]

There is more than just a symbolic connection between the physical heavens and the spiritual heavens in the Bible. In some passages, the stars of heaven are linked *interchangeably* with angelic heavenly beings, also referred to as "holy ones" or "sons of God" (Psa. 89:5-7; Job 1:6)[8]. Consider

---

[4] I. Zatelli, "Constellations." Toorn, K. van der, Bob Becking, and Pieter Willem van der Horst. *Dictionary of Deities and Demons in the Bible.* 2nd extensively rev. ed. Leiden; Boston; Grand Rapids, Mich.: Brill; Eerdmans, 1999., 202-204; "Astrology and the Worship of the Stars in the Bible," *ZAW* 103 (1991): 86-99.

[5] "Astrology", Berenbaum, Michael and Fred Skolnik, eds. 2nd ed. *Encyclopaedia Judaica.* Detroit: Macmillan Reference USA, 2007, p. 8424.

[6] See also Deut. 4:19; Deut. 17:3; 2 Kgs. 23:4-5; 1 Kgs. 22:19; Neh. 9:6.

[7] Tigay, Jeffrey. *JPS Torah Commentary: Deuteronomy.* Philadelphia: The Jewish Publication Society, 1996): 435; as quoted in Heiser, Michael S. "Deuteronomy 32:8 and the Sons of God," *Bibliotheca Sacra* 158 (January-March 2001): 72; Copyright © 2001 Dallas Theological Seminary; online: http://thedivinecouncil.com/

[8] See also Psa. 148:2-3, 1 Kgs. 22:29 & 2 Kgs. 21:5. In Isa. 14:12-14 the king of Babylon is likened to the planet Venus (Morningstar) seeking to reign above the other stars of heaven, which are equivalent to the sons of God who surround God's throne on the "mount of assembly" or "divine council" (see Psa. 89:5-7 and Psa. 82).

the following passages that equate the host of heaven with both astronomical bodies and angelic spirits *simultaneously*:

Job 38:4-7
"Where were you when I laid the foundation of the earth?...when the morning stars sang together and all the sons of God shouted for joy?"

Neh. 9:6
"You are the LORD, you alone. You have made heaven, the heaven of heavens, with all their host, the earth and all that is on it, the seas and all that is in them; and you preserve all of them; and the host of heaven worships you"

Dan. 8:10-11
"It grew great, even to the host of heaven. And some of the host and some of the stars it threw down to the ground and trampled on them. It became great, even as great as the Prince of the host [Michael]"

In these passages, we see the mythopoeic equivocation of sun, moon, and stars with heavenly angelic powers. But there is another symbolic connection made in the Old Testament of the sun, moon, and stars with earthly human authorities such as kings and rulers. It is as if these earthly principalities are empowered by or representative images of those spiritual beings and principalities.

In the passages below, notice that the destruction of earthly powers is expressed through the figurative language of a collapsing universe: The sky rolling up and the sun, moon, and stars being darkened or falling. Another way to describe this discourse is the language of "decreation."

Kings at war early 13th Century B.C.
Judg. 5:19-20
"The kings came, they fought... From heaven the stars fought, from their courses they fought against Sisera."

The destruction of Babylon in 539 B.C.

Isa. 13:10

"the stars of heaven and their constellations will not flash forth their light; The sun will be dark when it rises, And the moon will not shed its light."

The destruction of Edom in 586 B.C.

Isa. 34:4

"all the host of heaven will wear away, And the sky will be rolled up like a scroll; All their hosts will also wither away."

The destruction of Egypt in 587 B.C.

Ezek. 32:7

"When I blot you out, I will cover the heavens and make their stars dark; I will cover the sun with a cloud, and the moon shall not give its light. All the bright lights of heaven will I make dark over you, and put darkness on your land, declares the Lord GOD."

The destruction of Edom in 586 B.C.

Isa. 34:2-5

"For the LORD is enraged against all the nations, and furious against <u>all their host</u>; He has devoted them to destruction, has given them over for slaughter…All <u>the host of heaven</u> shall rot away, and <u>the skies roll up like a scroll</u>. All <u>their host shall fall</u>, as leaves fall.

During none of these historical events did the sky "literally" roll up or the stars fall or the sun and moon turn dark. These passages correlate the collapsing universe figuratively with the fall of earthly regimes and the spiritual powers behind them. Apologetic historical writing is embedded with mythopoeic imagery.

And this mythopoeic understanding is not a new invention. Eschatology expert Gary DeMar writes, "Before the advent of speculative exegesis, most

Bible commentators who studied the whole Bible understood the relationship of collapsing universe language with the destruction of the religious and civil state."[9] Scholar Kenneth L. Gentry adds, "In Scripture, prophets often express *national catastrophes* in terms of *cosmic destruction*. The famed twelfth-century Jewish theologian Maimonides notes that such language 'is a proverbial expression, importing the destruction and utter ruin of a nation.'"[10]

Perhaps some clarity can now be brought to the New Testament usage of the same exact imagery when describing the last days and the destruction of the Temple in Jerusalem.

> Matt. 24:29
>
> "Immediately after the tribulation of those days the sun will be darkened, and the moon will not give its light, and the stars will fall from heaven, and the powers of the heavens will be shaken."

> Rev. 6:12-14
>
> "When he opened the sixth seal, I looked, and behold, there was a great earthquake, and the sun became black as sackcloth, the full moon became like blood, and the stars of the sky fell to the earth as the fig tree sheds its winter fruit when shaken by a gale. The sky vanished like a scroll that is being rolled up, and every mountain and island was removed from its place"

Within the Church, there are several interpretations of when these prophesies are fulfilled, past, present, or future. But that does not concern us here. My main point is that these passages are so often used to look for a series of astronomical or geophysical catastrophes in creation, but now we see that they are actually a figurative expression rooted in Old Testament poetic imagery of the fall of ruling powers.

---

[9] DeMar, Gary. *Last Days Madness: Obsession of the Modern Church.* Powder Springs, GA: American Vision, 1999, p. 144.

[10] Ice, Thomas and Kenneth L. Gentry Jr. *The Great Tribulation Debate: Past or Future?* Grand Rapids, MI: Kregel, 1999, p. 55.

What I will argue next is that in the New Testament, the usage of these images denotes more than just ruling powers being vanquished, it figuratively depicts the end of the old covenant order itself.

The Last Days

The term "last days" comes from several New Testament passages (Acts 2:17-21; 2 Tim. 3:1; Heb. 1:2; Jas. 5:3; 2 Pet. 3:3), but the one that encapsulates the issues addressed in this chapter is Acts 2:17-21:

> "'And in the last days it shall be, God declares,
> that I will pour out my Spirit on all flesh,
> and your sons and your daughters shall prophesy,
> and your young men shall see visions,
> and your old men shall dream dreams;
> even on my male servants and female servants
> in those days I will pour out my Spirit, and they shall
> prophesy.
> And I will show wonders in the heavens above
> and signs on the earth below,
> blood, and fire, and vapor of smoke;
> the sun shall be turned to darkness
> and the moon to blood,
> before the day of the Lord comes, the great and magnificent
> day.
> And it shall come to pass that everyone who calls upon the
> name of the Lord shall be saved.'"

This passage seems to have it all: Day of the Lord, last days, wonders in heaven and earth. But let's take a closer look. This is an Old Testament prophecy that the apostle Peter is quoting to a large crowd of Jews and devout believers from all over the known world gathered in Jerusalem for the Day of Pentecost. He is preaching one of the first recorded salvation sermons on the resurrection of Jesus Christ and the need for all men everywhere to repent and be baptized in light of God's coming judgment.

The question arises: Is this "Day of the Lord," or "last days," something yet to occur in the distant future, a part of the end of the space-time universe? Is it the beginning of a series of momentous geophysical catastrophes including astronomical phenomena like a blood red moon and an eclipsed or darkened sun? As indicated earlier, most New Testament imagery is rooted in Old Testament concepts, so let's take a look at the Old Testament background for this concept of "the last days" in order to understand what the New Testament writers intended with their words.

First off, in the Old Testament, the "Day of the Lord" never meant the end of history or the destruction of the physical heavens and earth. It was used in varying contexts to proclaim God's judgment upon a specific city or nation. It was like saying "your day is coming when God will punish you."

Obadiah prophesied the destruction of Edom as *the day of the Lord* (Obad. 15), judgment on Judah and Jerusalem in the time of Zephaniah was called *the day of the Lord* (Zeph. 1:7, 14), Amos called the Assyrian destruction of the northern tribes *the day of the Lord* (Amos 5:18-20), Isaiah called the fall of Babylon to the Medes *the day of the Lord* (Isa. 13:6, 9). So when we read of "the Day of the Lord" in the New Testament, we must be careful not to expand it into an end of the universe scenario as we might think, but to understand it in context as coming earthly judgment upon a nation or people.[11]

The Old Testament precedent for "last days" is translated in some English Bibles as "latter days." In some instances it simply meant events that would happen years later from when the subject was addressed (Num. 24:14; Job 8:7). But with the prophets it became an eschatological reference about the children of Israel some day returning from exile and renewing the Kingdom of David, the archetype of Messiah, whose kingdom would be eternal after crushing the four previous kingdoms of Nebuchadnezzar's dream statue (Dan. 2:28; 10:14; Hos. 3:5).

---

[11] In 2 Thes. 2:2, Paul exhorts the Thessalonians not to believe anyone who says that the Day of the Lord has come. But he doesn't make the obvious rebuttal of saying "because it would be the end of the universe, duh." Instead he gives them other events that will happen first, thus proving that the Day of the Lord was a localized event not a universal or global one. If it was universal or global, they could not possibly be deceived into missing it. See Isa. 34:8, 35:4 in conjunction with Luke 21:22ff and Matt. 21:33-43. In these passages, the destruction of Jerusalem in A.D. 70 was the "days of vengeance" of God upon Israel for rejecting Messiah. "Days of vengeance" is a synonym for "Day of the Lord."

The "stone cut from a mountain by no human hand" (Dan. 2:35) that would crush the other successive kingdoms has been long known to be the "cornerstone" of God's Kingdom: Messiah, Jesus Christ (Isa. 28:16; Acts 4:11). That cornerstone that toppled the kingdoms of man came during the Roman Empire, the kingdom of iron mixed with clay in the First Century (Dan. 2:40-45). Daniel then says that, "the stone that struck the image became a great mountain and filled the whole earth" (2:35).

So now the question is, when does this mountain begin filling the earth? The prophets Isaiah and Micah further explain that "in the last days, the mountain of the house of the Lord shall be established as the highest of the mountains and many nations shall come, and say: "Come, let us go up to the mountain of the LORD, to the house of the God of Jacob" (Isa. 2:2-3; Mic. 4:1-2).

When do the nations begin coming to the mountain of the Lord? Are these last days at the Second Coming of Christ at the end of time or is this a figurative reference to the spread of the Gospel after the first coming of Christ? In their book *The Early Church and the End of the World*, scholars Gary DeMar and Francis Gumerlock list early church scholars such as Justin Martyr, Irenaeus, Tertullian, and others who understood Isaiah 2/Micah 4 and other Old Testament prophecies to be about the first coming of Christ rather than the second coming.[12] But don't take early church scholars' word for it. The New Testament apostles clearly claimed that they were in fact living in "the last days."

If we return to Peter's sermon in Acts 2, and read it in context we see from the very start that Peter claims that the mysterious tongues speaking that the crowd was hearing was in fact the fulfillment of the Joel prophecy about God pouring out His Spirit *in the last days* (Acts 2:16). This Pentecost event, with its explicit proclamation of the Kingdom of God in the various tongues of the nations, marked the beginning of that drawing in of the

---

[12] DeMar, Gary and Francis Gumerlock. *The Early Church and the End of the World*. Powder Springs, GA: American Vision, 2006, pp. xi-xiii. Among other important scholars who held this preterist interpretation of the last days or "end of the world" (especially of Matt. 24) were St. John Chrysostom, Bede, Eusebius, Augustine, Origen, Hugo Grotius, John Lightfoot, Milton Terry, Moses Stuart, John Calvin, Philip Dodderidge, Thomas Newton, John Gill, Adam Clarke, and F.W. Farrar.

nations to the Mountain of God, Messiah and the New Covenant (Heb. 12:22-24).

But Peter did not stop with the prophesying, dreams, and visions. He also included — in that current day fulfillment — the astronomical catastrophic phenomena of the sun, moon and stars which we now know are references to falling principalities and powers both earthly and heavenly. Peter claims that those prophecies were being fulfilled *in their very day,* not in some distant end of the universe. And Peter reiterates his belief of being in "these last times" (1 Pet. 1:10) when he claims in his letters that "the end of all things is at hand" (1 Pet. 4:7), not in some distant future.

But Peter was not the only one who explicitly proclaimed their era as the "last days." Both Peter and Paul referred to the scoffers and depraved people *of their own time* to be a sign that they were in the last days in the first century (2 Pet. 3:1-4; 2 Tim. 3:1-9). Paul wrote to the Corinthian church that they were the generation "on whom the end of the ages has come" (1 Cor. 10:11), the same generation that Jesus said would see the destruction of the Temple that occurred in A.D. 70 (Matt. 23:36; 24:34). The writer of Hebrews said conclusively that "Long ago, at many times and in many ways, God spoke to our fathers by the prophets, but in *these last days* He has spoken to us by His Son" (Heb. 1:1-2).

So if the New Testament writers believed they were living in the last days, then what could that concept mean if not the last days of the space-time universe? As I will explain in the next section, I think the cosmic language of the Bible indicates that they believed they were living in the last days of the Old Covenant and the beginning days of the New Covenant. And in a further concluding section I will explain why this interpretation does not necessarily deny a Second Coming of Christ. You'll have to bear with me.

Shaking the Heavens and Earth

In chapter 2, "Biblical Creation and Storytelling," I argued that the establishment of covenants by God is spoken of in the Bible in figurative terms of the creation of the heavens and earth. After all, the Jews' entire existence and reality was interpreted through their covenant with God, so it makes perfect ancient Near Eastern sense to speak of it in the big picture terms of heaven and earth.

God describes the creation of His covenant with Moses as the creation of the heavens and the earth (Isa. 51:14-16). The creation of Israel through deliverance and Promised Land was likened to God hovering over the waters and filling the formless and void earth (Deut. 32:10-12), separating the waters from the dry land (Exod. 15:8, 16-17), establishing the sun and moon, and defeating the mythical sea dragon of chaos to create His ordered world (Psa. 74:12-17; 89:6-12; Isa. 51:9-14).

If the creation of a covenant is spoken of as the creation of heavens and earth, and the ruling powers are referred to as sun, moon and stars, then what would the destruction of those powers be but the destruction of the heavens and the earth, including the fall of those astronomical symbolic entities? And what was the embodiment of that covenant but the holy Temple in the holy city of King David?

The first time that Jerusalem and the Temple was destroyed in 586 B.C. by the Babylonians, the prophets used the language of decreation to express the covenantal violation of Israel. The destruction of the Temple and exile of the Jews through God's providence was likened to the destruction of the heavens and earth and a return to a pre-creation chaotic state, a reversal of Genesis 1 language:

> Jer. 4:23-26
>
> I looked on the earth, and behold, it was <u>without form and void</u>;
> and to the <u>heavens</u>, and they <u>had no light</u>.
> I looked on the <u>mountains</u>, and behold, they <u>were quaking,</u>
> I looked, and behold, there was <u>no man,</u>
> and all the <u>birds</u> of the air <u>had fled</u>.
> I looked, and behold, the fruitful land was a <u>desert</u>...
> For this the earth shall mourn,
> and the heavens above be dark.

Isa. 24:1-23

Behold, the LORD will empty the earth and make it desolate...

The earth shall be utterly empty and utterly plundered...

The earth staggers like a drunken man;

On that day the LORD will punish

the host of heaven, in heaven,

and the kings of the earth, on the earth...

Then the moon will be confounded

and the sun ashamed.

In the same way that the first temple destruction was earth shattering in its covenantal impact, so the second destruction of Jerusalem and the holy Temple in A.D. 70 was of equal spiritual significance in God's covenantal relations with Israel. It was the shaking of the heavens and earth with a punishment of the host of heaven, both astronomical and political/spiritual. This is a perfect example of C.S. Lewis' "myth become fact," an apologetic of God's Word being true.

In the year A.D. 66, revolutionary Zealots and other factions had fueled a revolt against their Roman occupiers. The leaders of Israel had rejected Jesus of Nazareth as being the Messiah, but they knew the calculations of Daniel's prophecy (Dan. 9:24-27). The 490 years were up. Messiah would arrive, crush the Roman pagan oppressors and establish the long awaited eternal Kingdom of God (Dan. 2:44-45) on earth.

The Roman emperor Nero sent his general Vespasian to crush the Jewish rebellion and bring peace back to Roman rule. The city of Jerusalem was besieged by Vespasian's son Titus, and by the summer of A.D. 70, was completely destroyed, along with the Jewish Temple. A million or more Jews were killed, a hundred thousand were made slaves and exiled,[13] and the Temple has never since been rebuilt from its ruins.

This important piece of history was extensively recorded by a Jewish historian in the Roman court, Flavius Josephus, in his book *The Wars of the Jews*. In this single historical event lies the key to understanding many

---

[13] Flavius Josephus. *Wars of the Jews*, 6.9.3 (6:420).

mysterious metaphors and perplexing poetry of end times apocalyptic. What appears to modern Americans as esoteric Nostradamus-like riddles in Biblical language about the "end of the age," when interpreted through the images and metaphors of the Old Testament, becomes a powerful mythopoeic testimony of the New Covenant.

This all sheds light on Jesus' prophecy about the impending destruction of the Jerusalem Temple when He was asked by His disciples on the Mount of Olives, "Tell us, when will these things happen, and what will be the sign of Your coming, and of the end of the age?" (Matt. 24:3).

The Greek word for "age" is not *cosmos* as in the physical world, but *aion*, as in a time era. Jesus was not describing the end of the space-time universe, He was talking about the end of the Old Covenant era, the last days of the Old Covenant that culminated in the destruction of the sacramental incarnation of that Old Covenant: The Temple in Jerusalem (Matt. 24:1-2).

As scholar N.T. Wright put it,

> "The 'close of the age' for which they longed was not the end of the space-time order, but the end of the present evil age, and the introduction of the (still very much this-worldly) age to come... Matthew 24:3, therefore is most naturally read, in its first-century Jewish context... as a question of Jesus 'coming' or 'arriving' in the sense of his actual enthronement as king, consequent upon the dethronement of the present powers that were occupying the holy city...When will the evil age, symbolized by the present Jerusalem regime, be over?"[14]

The destruction of the Old Covenant order would be likened to the destruction of the heavens and the earth.

In Hebrews 12:18-22, the writer tells us that God shook the heavens and the earth when He established His covenant with Moses on Sinai. But then in verses 23-24 he says that the New Covenant is a heavenly city of God on the Mount Zion of the heavenly Jerusalem, far superior to the Mosaic covenant.

---

[14] Wright, N.T. *Jesus and the Victory of God*. Minneapolis, MN: Fortress Press, 1996, p. 345-346.

Then he concludes that the end of that Old Covenant is near because a new shaking of the heavens and earth is coming, and that shaking is the establishment of the New Covenant.

> Heb. 12:26-28
> At that time His voice shook the earth, but now He has promised, "Yet once more I will shake not only the earth but also the heavens." This phrase, "Yet once more," indicates the removal of things that are shaken — that is, things that have been made — in order that the things that cannot be shaken may remain. Therefore let us be grateful for receiving a kingdom that cannot be shaken.

J. Stuart Russell answers the relevant question, "What then, is the great catastrophe symbolically represented as the shaking of the earth and heavens?"

> "No doubt it is the overthrow and abolition of the Mosaic dispensation, or old covenant; the destruction of the Jewish church and state, together with all the institutions and ordinances connect therewith... the laws, and statutes, and ordinances."[15]

The book of Hebrews was written before A.D. 70, when the Temple was destroyed. So the physical embodiment of the Old Covenant was still on earth even though the New Covenant had been inaugurated by the death and resurrection of Christ. It was not until the Temple was destroyed that the New Covenant was considered fully inaugurated. They were living in a transition period between covenants during the years of AD 30-70.

This is why the writer of Hebrews says, "In speaking of a new covenant, He makes the first one obsolete. And what is becoming obsolete and growing old is ready to vanish away" (Heb. 8:13). Notice how the author says that the Old Covenant was becoming old and obsolete but was not yet

---

[15] Russell, J. Stuart. *The Parousia: The New Testament Doctrine of Our Lord's Second Coming.* Grand Rapids, MI: Baker, 1999, p. 289.

replaced. That is because the incarnation of the old heavens and earth, the Jerusalem Temple, was not yet destroyed at the time of his writing. The Old Covenant was the heavens and earth that was shaken and replaced by the New Covenant, which is the eternal kingdom that will never be replaced or shaken.

The Day of the Lord in 2 Peter

2 Pet. 3:10–13
But the day of the Lord will come like a thief, and then the heavens will pass away with a roar, and the elements will be burned up and dissolved, and the earth and the works that are done on it will be exposed…
Since all these things are thus to be dissolved, what sort of people ought you to be in lives of holiness and godliness, waiting for and hastening the coming of the day of God, because of which the heavens will be set on fire and dissolved, and the elements will melt as they burn! But according to His promise we are waiting for new heavens and a new earth in which righteousness dwells.

The interpretation I have presented in this essay is no doubt earth shattering for some eschatological paradigms about the end times. Such radical departures from the futurist's received wisdom always begs plenty of questions about other passages and concepts taken for granted by the futurist interpretation.

One of them is the apparently clear description in 2 Peter about the day of the Lord and the passing away of the heavens and the earth replaced by a new heavens and earth. Isn't that unambiguous language to be taken literally? Well, actually, no. As a matter of fact, orthodox believers have wide ranging interpretations of this passage, so it is a controversial one to begin with.[16]

---

[16] Bauckham, Richard J. Vol. 50, *Word Biblical Commentary: 2 Peter, Jude.* Word Biblical Commentary. Dallas: Word, Incorporated, 2002, p. 315-319.

We must remember our dictum to seek to understand the text within its ancient Jewish setting steeped in Old Testament imagery and symbols. I believe when we do this, we will have to conclude that the decreation of the heavens and earth is covenantal mythopoeia, *not* literal physical scientific observation. Peter writes figuratively about the final ending of the Old Covenant, with God's judgment on Israel for rejecting Messiah, and the final establishment of His New Covenant as a New World Order, or in their case, a "new heavens and new earth."

In the beginning of chapter 3, Peter compares the scoffers of his day and their impending judgment with the scoffers of Noah's day before their judgment. So the judgment is near, and what's more, these scoffers are in the "last days" which we have already seen were considered the last days of the Old Covenant that the New Testament writers were living within. Those last days would be climaxed by judgment. But what kind of judgment?

Peter references creation of the heavens and earth (red flag about covenants!) and then the destruction of that previous world by water. Scholars have indicated how the flood of Noah is described using terms similar to Genesis 1, as if God is "decreating" the earth because of sin, in order to start over with a new Noahic covenant.[17] The ark floated over the chaotic "face of the waters" (Gen. 7:17) like God's spirit hovered over the chaotic face of the waters before creation (Gen. 1:2). The dry land recedes from the waters (8:3) just as it was separated in creation (1:9). God makes the same command to Noah to be fruitful and multiply and fill the earth (9:1) that He gave to Adam and Eve (1:28). So the covenantal connections are loud and clear.

As already noted, the Day of the Lord is always used in the Bible for a localized judgment upon a people, which by way of reminder, Jesus had already prophesied was coming upon Jerusalem to the very generation He spoke to (Matt. 23:36-24:2). But what makes some interpreters think this is the final judgment of the universe is the very bad translation of the Greek word *stoicheion* as "elements" in some English texts. This makes modern readers think of the periodic table of elements as being the most foundational building blocks of the universe. They conclude that the Bible must be talking

---

[17]Wenham, Gordon J. Vol. 1, *Word Biblical Commentary: Genesis 1-15*. Word Biblical Commentary. Dallas: Word, Incorporated, 2002, p. 207.

about the very elements of helium, hydrogen, deuterium and others being burned up and melted!

But this is not what the Greek word means. Though some Greek thinkers believed in the existence of atoms, the common understanding was that there were four basic elements — earth, water, wind, and fire.[18] Though someone may conjecture that these could still be considered physical elements that could be destroyed, a simple look at the usage of *stoicheion* throughout the New Testament shows that the Hebrew usage had nothing to do with Greek primitive scientific notions.

In every place that *stoicheion* shows up in the New Testament it means elementary principle rudiments of a worldview, sometimes a godless worldview (Col. 2:8), but more often the elementary principles of the Old Covenant law described as a "cosmos" (Gal. .4:3; 9; Col. 2:20; Heb. 5:12).[19]

Remember how the cosmic language of creating heavens and earth was used to describe the cosmic significance of God establishing a covenant? And remember how in the Old Testament, the destruction of covenants, nations, and peoples was described in *decreation* terms as the collapsing of the universe?

That is the case in these passages as well, with the term "cosmos" being used metaphorically for the "universe" of God's covenantal order as embodied in the Old Covenant laws of Jewish separation: Circumcision, dietary restrictions and sabbaths. Paul is telling his readers that the *stoicheion* of the Old Covenant *cosmos* are no longer over them because the people of God are under new *stoicheion*, the elementary principles of faith (Gal. 4:1-11).

Peter means the same thing. When he says that the heavens will pass away and the *stoicheion* will be burned up, he is claiming that when the Temple in Jerusalem is destroyed, it will be the final passing away of the Old Covenant cosmos, along with all the elementary principles tied to that

---

[18] Schreiner, Thomas R. Vol. 37, *1, 2 Peter, Jude*. electronic ed. Logos Library System; The New American Commentary. Nashville: Broadman & Holman Publishers, 2007, p. 384.

[19] Leithart, Peter J. *The Promise of His Appearing: An Exposition of Second Peter*. Moscow, ID: Canon Press, 2004, p.101. Bauckham argues that "The heavenly bodies (sun, moon and stars) is the interpretation favored by most commentators," for *stoicheion*. But then we are right back to the sun, moon, and stars as figurative language of covenantal elements. Bauckham, *2 Peter, Jude*, 316. But I doubt this interpretation because the clear words for "heavenly bodies" are not *stoicheion*, but *epouranios soma* (1 Cor. 15:40-41).

physical sacramental structure, the laws that once separated Jew and Gentile. The new cosmos is one in which both Jew and Gentile "by God's power are being guarded through faith for a salvation ready to be revealed in the last time" (1 Pet. 1:5).

As Gary DeMar concludes, "The New Covenant replaces the Old Covenant with new leaders, a new priesthood, new sacraments, a new sacrifice, a new tabernacle (John 1:14), and a new temple (John 2:19; 1 Cor. 3:16; Eph. 2:21). In essence, a new heaven and earth."[20] Eminent Greek scholar John Lightfoot agrees, "The destruction of Jerusalem and the whole Jewish state is described as if the whole frame of this world were to be dissolved."[21]

The new heavens and new earth in which righteousness dwells that Peter was waiting for was the New Covenant cosmos of righteousness by faith inaugurated by Christ's death and resurrection. That New Covenant inauguration and implementation was not merely an abstract claim of contractual change, it was physically verified with the destruction of the Old Covenant emblem, the Temple, that finalized the dissolution of the Old Covenant itself.

> Matt. 23:36-38
>
> "O Jerusalem, Jerusalem, the city that kills the prophets and stones those who are sent to it! How often would I have gathered your children together as a hen gathers her brood under her wings, and you would not! See, your house [Temple] is left to you desolate.
>
> Truly, I say to you, all these things will come upon this generation.

Coming on the Clouds

Jesus' Olivet Discourse in Matthew 24 is the classic reference used by futurists to point to the future second coming of Christ. I have been

---

[20] Gary DeMar, *Last Days Madness,* p. 192.

[21] Lightfoot, John. *Commentary on the New Testament from the Talmud and Hebraica: Matthew – 1 Corinthians,* 4 vols. Peabody, MA: Hendrickson, 1859, 1989, 3:454.

exegeting the decreation language about the sun, moon, and stars as referring to the end of the Old Covenant. Yet, right after those verses that speak of the collapsing universe, Jesus speaks of His "coming on the clouds":

> Matt. 24:29-30
>
> "Immediately after the tribulation of those days the sun will be darkened, and the moon will not give its light, and the stars will fall from heaven, and the powers of the heavens will be shaken. Then will appear in heaven the sign of the Son of Man, and then all the tribes of the land will mourn, and they will see the Son of Man coming on the clouds of heaven with power and great glory."

I want to focus on the phrase, "coming on the clouds of heaven" to prove that it is not the physical return of Christ, but rather a metaphor for God's judgment upon Jerusalem for rejecting Messiah. I believe Jesus Christ will physically return to this earth, but I do not think that this passage teaches that doctrine. It teaches something else. And I am in good company with orthodox scholars through history who have posited this very interpretation of Matthew 24; Eusebius, John Calvin, John Lightfoot, John Gill, Phillip Schaff, Gary DeMar, Kenneth L. Gentry, R.C. Sproul and many others.[22]

When considering the ancient Near Eastern context of this "cloud" image, I have previously written that the notion of deity coming on clouds or riding clouds like a chariot was already a powerful metaphor used of the god Baal in Canaan when Israel arrived there. Baal, the storm god, was called the great "Cloud-Rider"[23] who would dispense his judgments through thunder and lightning in his hand.[24] To ride the clouds was a sign of deity and judgment to

---

[22] DeMar, Gary. *End Times Fiction: A Biblical Consideration of the Left Behind Theology.* Nashville, TN: Thomas Nelson, 2001, 111-115. For more, see "Preterist Scholarship" on the Preterist Archive: http://www.preteristarchive.com/Preterism/index.html.

[23] KTU 1.2:4.8–9; 1.3:3.38–41. All these Ugaritic texts can be found in N. Wyatt, *Religious Texts from Ugarit*, 2nd ed., The Biblical Seminar, vol. 53 (London: Sheffield Academic Press, 2002).

[24] Baal sits...
in the midst of his divine mountain, Saphon,
in the midst of the mountain of victory.

the Canaanites. So it makes sense that the Biblical writers who were dispossessing Baal and his worshippers from the land would use the same epithets of Yahweh in a subversive way of saying Yahweh is God, not Baal.

In light of this connection of cloud-riding with deity and judgment, Jesus' statement becomes an implicit reference to His own deity and Messiahship rejected by the first century Jews which resulted in God's judgment upon Jerusalem (Matt. 21:33-45). Jesus is coming in judgment to vindicate His claims (Matt. 26:64), and He is going to do so by using the Roman armies of Titus to do His bidding.

Look at these Old Testament passages that use the concept of coming on the clouds as a metaphor for God coming in judgment upon cities or nations:[25]

God's judgment on Egypt

Isa. 19:1

Behold, the LORD is <u>riding on a swift cloud</u>, and is about to come to Egypt.

Ezek. 30:3

For the day is near, the day of the LORD is near; it will be a <u>day of clouds</u>, a <u>time of doom</u> for the nations.

Seven lightning-flashes,
eight bundles of thunder,
a tree-of-lightning in his right hand.
His head is magnificent,
His brow is dew-drenched.
his feet are eloquent in wrath.
(KTU 1.101:1–6)
The season of his rains may Baal indeed appoint,
the season of his storm-chariot.
And the sound of his voice from the clouds,
his hurling to the earth of lightning-flashes
(KTU 1.4:5.5–9)
[25] See also Psa. 18:9-10; 68:32-33; 104:3; 2 Sam. 22:10; Zeph. 1:15; Isa. 30:30-31 cf 31:15; Deut. 33:26.

God's judgment on Ninevah

Nah. 1:3

In whirlwind and storm is His way, And clouds are the dust beneath His feet.

God's judgment on Israel

Joel 2:2

Surely it is near, A day of darkness and gloom, A day of <u>clouds and thick darkness</u>.

Messiah as deity and kingly judge

Dan. 7:13-14

"I kept looking in the night visions, And behold, <u>with the clouds of heaven</u> One like a Son of Man was coming, And He <u>came up</u> to the Ancient of Days And was presented before Him. And to Him was given dominion, Glory and a kingdom."

Did God literally or physically come riding on a cumulus nimbus in these passages? The answer is obvious: No. The notion of coming on the clouds with storm and lightning was an ancient Near Eastern motif of deity coming in judgment upon a city or nation. Egypt was plundered by the Assyrians (Isa. 9:23-25). Ninevah was destroyed by the hand of Nebuchadnezzar of Babylon (Ezek. 30:10). But God is described as the one who was using these pagan forces as His own means of judging those cities. This is how God "came on the clouds."

So Matthew 24 is God's description of judging Israel for rejecting Messiah by using the Roman armies to destroy the Temple and Jerusalem. Jesus didn't physically come riding on a cumulus nimbus, He "came on the clouds" in judgment by using the Roman armies to vindicate His claims of Messiahship. This was not a physical Second Coming, but a spiritual coming.

Once it is realized that creation and decreation language regarding the heavens and the earth is covenantal in its reference, and not scientific, the natural question arises, does this deny the second coming of Christ altogether? Is this a heterodox view that leads us on the slippery slope into heresy? My answer is again, "no."

Context is everything. Just because *some* passages are shown to be fulfilled in the past, does not mean that *all* passages are fulfilled in the past. For example, many preterists maintain that 1 Corinthians 15 affirms that there will be a future physical return of Christ followed by a physical resurrection of humanity.

> 1 Cor. 15:20-26
>
> But in fact Christ has been raised from the dead, the firstfruits of those who have fallen asleep. For as by a man came death, by a man has come also the resurrection of the dead. For as in Adam all die, so also in Christ shall all be made alive. But each in his own order: Christ the firstfruits, then at His coming those who belong to Christ. Then comes the end, when He delivers the kingdom to God the Father after destroying every rule and every authority and power. For He must reign until He has put all His enemies under His feet. The last enemy to be destroyed is death.

Other preterists make the argument that the "new creation" and "new heavens and earth" of the New Covenant may have been inaugurated in the first century, but it will not be consummated until this physical return of Christ. At that time, what was a spiritual truth of new creation will become a physical reality. Christ reigns now over every authority and power (Eph. 1:20-22). But His overcoming of every authority and power is a process that is not yet completed (Heb. 2:8). This notion of a seed form of beginning with a future completion is referred to as the "Now/Not Yet" of the Kingdom of God. As scholar Ken Gentry writes,

> "Despite initial appearances, Revelation 21-22 does not speak of the consummate new creation order. Rather, it provides an ideal conception of new covenant Christianity, presenting it as the spiritual new creation and the new Jerusalem. Though the ultimate, consummate, eternal new

creation is implied in these verses, (via the now/not yet schema of New Testament revelation), John's actual focus is on the current, unfolding, redemptive new creation principle in Christ."[26]

This now/not yet, inauguration/consummation paints a picture of a New Covenant that is already here with a new creation of a new heavens and earth that will one day be fully consummated at the physical return of Christ and the resurrection of the dead. At that time, Death will be swallowed up in victory, even though we can now speak of it having already lost its sting. This is present reality based on future promise.

> 1 Cor. 15:54-57
> When the perishable puts on the imperishable, and the mortal puts on immortality, then shall come to pass the saying that is written:
> "Death is swallowed up in victory."
> "O death, where is your victory?
> O death, where is your sting?"
> The sting of death is sin, and the power of sin is the law. But thanks be to God, who gives us the victory through our Lord Jesus Christ.

---

[26] Gentry, Kenneth L. Jr. *Navigating the Book of Revelation: Special Studies on Important Issues.* Fountain Inn: SC, Goodbirth Ministries, 2009, p. 167.

CHAPTER 7

An Apologetic of Biblical Horror

This chapter has been adapted from the article, "An Apologetic of Horror" in the Christian Research Journal Vol. 32 / No. 04 (2009).

When one thinks of horror movies, the usual images conjured up in the mind are of nubile coeds being lured to isolated locations for the purpose of having sex and then being murdered and carved up in ever innovative and disgusting new ways by a grotesque chimera or phantasm. Likewise, for thriller movies, images that stalk the mind are of innocent men or women being hunted by maniacal serial murderers as a relentless feast of fear and gore for the audience.

Though these repulsive clichés have become the norm for many Hollywood horror and thriller films, they are not the only approach to the genres. In fact, in today's postmodern society so saturated with relative morality, horror and thriller stories have the ability to be an effective apologetic for the Christian worldview.

Some well-meaning cultural crusaders make claims that horror is an intrinsically evil genre that is not appropriate for Christians to create or enjoy. They believe horror is an unbiblical genre of storytelling. One writer argues, "Horror is an example of a genre which was conceived in rebellion. It is based on a fascination with ungodly fear. It should not be imitated, propagated, or encouraged. It cannot be redeemed because it is presuppositionally at war with God."[1] Evidently, God disagrees with such religious critics because God Himself told horror stories thousands of years before Stephen King or Wes Craven were even born.

The prophet Daniel wrote horror literature, based on images and drama cinematically displayed by God Himself in Babylon. Not only did God turn

---

[1] Doug Phillips, Doug's Blog, November 1, 2006, "The Horror Genre," http://www.visionforum.com/hottopics/blogs/dwp/2006/11/1878.asp.

the blaspheming king Nebuchadnezzar into an insane wolfman to humble his idolatrous pride (Dan. 4), but He storyboarded horror epics for kings Belshazzar and Darius as allegories of the historical battle between good and evil to come. Huge hybrid carnivorous monsters come out of the sea like Godzilla, one of them with large fangs and ravishing claws to devour, crush, and trample over the earth (7:1–8) until it is slain and its flesh roasted in fire (7:11); there are blasphemous sacrileges causing horror (8:13), including an abomination of desolation (9:26–27), angels and demons engaging in warfare (10:13), rivers of fire (7:10), deep impact comets and meteors colliding with the earth, *Armageddon* style (8:10), wars, desolation, and complete destruction (9:26-27). The book of Daniel reads like God's own horror film festival.

It is not merely the human being Daniel who crafted this work of epic horror allegory, it is *God Himself* who rolled the camera and directed the action. God Himself enjoys the horror genre. That's God-breathed inerrancy. The author of this faith didn't grow out of it after the Old Testament. In fact, He may have received an even harsher movie rating in His later production, the New Testament.

The book of Revelation is an epic horror fantasy sequel to Daniel, complete with science fiction special effects, and spectacles of horror darker than anything in a David Cronenberg Grand Guignol theater of blood. In this apocalyptic prophecy we read of a huge demonic spectacle of genetically mutated monsters chasing and tormenting screaming people (9:1–11), armies of bizarre beasts wreaking death and destruction on the masses (9:13–18), a demonic dragon chasing a woman with the intent to eat her child (12:3–4), a seven-headed amphibious Hydra with horns that blasphemes God and draws pagan idol worship from everyone on earth (13:1–10), massive famines (6:8), gross outbreaks of rotting sores covering people's bodies (16:2), plagues of demonic insects torturing populations (9:1–11), fire-breathing Griffon-like creatures (9:17), supernatural warfare of angels and demons (12:7), the dragging of rotting corpses through the streets while people party over them (11:7–13), rivers and seas of blood (14:20; 16:3), a blaspheming harlot doing the deed with kings and merchants (17:1-5) who then turn on her, strip her naked, burn her with fire, and cannibalize her (17:16), more famines, pestilence and plagues (18:8), and when the good guys win, there is a mighty feast of vultures scavenging the flesh of kings and commanders in victory (19:17–18). And I might add, this all gives glory to God in the highest.

The prophetic and apocalyptic genres that were used by the prophets and apostles of God relied heavily on images of horror to solicit holy fear of sin and its consequences in their audience and point them to God. Horror and thriller movies (and by extension, other forms of horror storytelling or image-making) can accomplish this same "prophetic" redemptive task several ways.

Original Sin Crouching at the Door

First, horror can be redemptive by reinforcing the doctrine of man's sinful nature. Gothic storytelling prides itself on exploiting man's fear of his dark side through vampires, werewolves, and other half-man/half-monsters. These freaks of nature or supernature personify the cultured, educated man by day and the unbridled beast by night. They represent the gospel truth that our evil nature avoids the light, lest its deeds be exposed (John 3:20), and that true evil is done by otherwise "normal" people who suppress the truth about themselves in unrighteousness (Rom. 1:18–21). We are Jekylls and Hydes, all.

The Victorian era provided western culture with a rich and lasting heritage of Christian metaphors for the depraved side of human nature that requires restraint. Those metaphors have been resurrected in some modern films with equal moral vision. *Dracula* symbolized the struggle of the repressed dark side and its eternal hunger and need for redemption, which is explored with modern fervor in *Interview with the Vampire* and *Dracula 2000*.[2] Dr. Jekyll fought to suppress the increasing inhumanity of his depraved alter ego, Mr. Hyde, just like Jack has to defeat his destructive

---

[2] The unique twist in *Dracula 2000* is in its depiction of Dracula's origins. Dracula is revealed to be the undead soul of Judas Iscariot prowling the earth in vengeance against his own perdition. This story contains strong Christian metaphors: Dracula/Judas's insatiable lust for blood is a symbol of the eternal need for Christ's blood of forgiveness; the silver abhorrence, a reflection of the thirty pieces Judas betrayed Christ for, and of course, crosses and wooden stakes through the heart, elements of the power of the cross of Christ to destroy evil. *Dracula 2000* resurrects Christian elements that have been buried by many contemporary vampire movies.

inner self, Tyler Durden in *Fight Club*. Victor Frankenstein's scientific hubris leads to a vengeful monster in the same way that the conceit of scientists without moral restraint leads to the takeover of Jurassic Park by unpredictable dinosaurs. The corrupted conscience of H.G. Wells' Invisible Man getting away with crime is revisited in the more recent *Hollow Man*.

One movie, *The Addiction,* uses the vampire genre as a metaphor for the addictive sinful nature of humanity. The vampires spout human philosophy as they kill their victims, attempting to prove there is no moral authority to condemn what they do. One of them even concedes R.C. Sproul's theological point, that, "we're not sinners because we sin, we sin because we are sinners." One victim is shocked at being bitten by her friend. She anxiously blurts out, "How could you do this? Doesn't it affect you? How can you do this to me?" To which her vampiress friend sardonically replies, "It was your decision. Your friend Feuerbach said that all men counting stars are equivalent in every way to God. My indifference is not the concern here. It's your astonishment that needs study." This reversal is an apologetic argument against unbelief, par excellence. If God is dead, as the modern secular mindset proposes, and man is his own deity, creating his own morality, then no one should be surprised when people create their own morality by feasting on the blood of others. Ideas have consequences. Without God, there is no such thing as "evil." In the end, the vampiress, believe it or not, has a Catholic conversion! This film embodies the argument for God's existence through the existence of evil.[3]

Your Sin Will Find You Out

Another way in which horror and thriller movies can communicate truth about human nature is in showing the logical consequences of sin. In the same way, the Bible plays out some sexually disgusting scenarios and gruesome violence in order to communicate the seriousness of sin and its negative impact upon our relationship with God.

In Ezekiel 16 and 23, God describes Israel's spiritual condition figuratively as a harlot "spreading her legs" to every Egyptian, Assyrian and

---

[3] Another vampire film that warns of the subtle and seductive nature of sin is *Let the Right One In*, a story of a young boy befriending a young girl who happens to be a vampire.

Chaldean who passes by, as well as donkeys (bestiality) and idols as sexual devices. The book of Judges depicts the horrors of a society where "every man does what is right in his own eyes," such as gang rapes and dismemberment (19:22-29), burning victims alive (9:49), cutting off thumbs (1:6-7), and disemboweling (3:21-22) among other monstrous atrocities that illustrate their need for repentance.

Hide and Seek is a story in the vein of Dr. Jekyll and Mr. Hyde about a man named David whose daughter is in danger from some kind of scary imaginary man who is stalking her. Like Nathan's parable to King David, this David learns that "he is that man," his dissociated split identity a symptom of his suppressed past sins.

The Machinist and *The Number 23* are both macabre Poe-like tales that illustrate the effect of suppressing sin and guilt, as well as the redemptive power of confession. *The Machinist* is about an industrial worker whose body and mind wastes away from insomnia because of his running away from a past crime. The movie is a literalization of Psalms 32:3–5: "When I kept silent about my sin, my body wasted away through my groaning all day long... I said, 'I will confess my transgressions to the LORD'; and Thou didst forgive the guilt of my sin. "

The Number 23 is a thriller about a guy whose discovery of a novel that mysteriously reflects his own life leads him to an obsession with the number twenty-three, which ultimately leads him into mental disorder that endangers others. It's not until he faces the fact that all the mysterious coincidences in his life are the bubbling up of suppressed sin and guilt that he can repent and find redemption. Not coincidentally, the filmmaker put a Bible verse at the end of the film to express this very theme: "Be sure your sin will find you out" (Num. 32:23).

Ghost stories have been a staple of humanity's storytelling diet since the beginning. From the Bible's witch of Endor, to Shakespeare's Hamlet, to modern campfire yarns, people love to tell ghost stories to scare the Beetlejuice out of each other. Christians sometimes condemn ghost stories because they seem to imply a purgatory that is not in the Bible, or because they appear to violate the Scriptural prohibition against calling up the dead. But the purpose of some ghost stories has nothing to do with "reality." They are often metaphors depicting morally "unfinished business" or the demand for justice against unsolved crime, very much in the Biblical spirit of the voice of Abel's murdered blood crying to God for justice from the ground (Gen. 4:10).

A Stir of Echoes, *The Haunting*, *Gothika*, and *The Haunting in Connecticut* are all movies where ghosts are not haunting people because they are evil, but because they are victims of unsolved murders who can't rest until the murderer pays for his crimes. These are parables communicating that there is no spiritual statute of limitations on the guilt of sin. They are fables about the telltale heart of moral conscience.

Some sincere Christians will often find Bible passages that in their eyes appear to discredit the narrative depiction of sin and its guilty consequences. One such common passage is Philippians 4:8:

> "Finally, brethren, whatever is true, whatever is honorable, whatever is right, whatever is pure, whatever is lovely, whatever is of good repute, if there is any excellence and if anything worthy of praise, dwell on these things."

Contrary to some interpretations, this passage does not depict Christianity as an episode of *Veggie Tales* or *Little House on the Prairie*. It is not only true, honorable and right to show the glorious blessings of the gospel. It is also true, honorable and right to show the intestines of Judas, the betrayer of that gospel, bursting out after hanging himself (Acts 1:18–19). It is not only pure, lovely and of good repute that Noah was depicted in the Bible as a righteous man, but it is also pure, lovely and of good repute that all the other inhabitants of the earth around him were depicted as entirely wicked and worthy of destruction (Gen. 6:5). It is not only excellent and worthy of praise that Lot was revealed as a righteous man, but it is also excellent and worthy of praise that the destroyed inhabitants of Sodom were revealed as unrighteous men "who indulge the flesh in its corrupt desires" (2 Pet. 2:10).

The portrayal of good *and* evil, as well as their consequences, are two sides of God's one honorable, pure, lovely, excellent, and praiseworthy truth. According to the Bible, pointing out wrong is part of dwelling on what is right, exposing lies is part of dwelling on the truth, revealing cowardice is part of dwelling on the honorable, and uncovering corruption is part of dwelling on the pure.

Monsters of Modernity: Hubris

Horror and thriller stories can also be redemptive when they illustrate the consequences of modern man's hubris. In his book, *Monsters from the Id*, Michael E. Jones writes about the origins of modern horror as a reaction to the Enlightenment worldview. Jones points out that the Enlightenment rejection of the supernatural, the exaltation of man's primary urges, and scientific hubris created Frankenstein, Dracula, Jekyll and Hyde, and others.[4] He argues that the evils of horror are the result of suppressing morality, which backfires on us in the form of the monsters it breeds.

Jones explains the origins of Frankenstein as author Mary Wollstonecraft Shelley's personal attempt to make sense out of the conflict between the Enlightenment's naturalism and sexual libertinism and the classical Christian moral order. Mary Wollstonecraft had been initiated into the inner circle of libertine poets Percy Shelley and Lord Byron. By the time Mary wrote her novel, she had married Shelley and experienced an avalanche of the consequences of living out Enlightenment sexual and political "liberation" with her husband: familial alienation, jealousy and betrayal, promiscuity, adultery, incest, psychosis, suicides, and drug abuse. These men espoused "nature" in place of morality and therefore behaved as animals. In the novel, Dr. Frankenstein is the symbol of enlightened man. He is the "hero" or high priest of the religion of science, the belief that man is ultimately a machine, reducible to chemistry and physics. His creation of the monster is his ultimate act of hubris in playing God. The monster's pursuit of vengeance against the doctor is a playing out of the miserable consequences Shelley herself had experienced in her own life.[5]

A common staple in many horror films is the calmly deliberate, logical-minded scientist who tortures or kills in the name of scientific therapy or advancement. The scientist's often flat affect or calm in the face of others'

---

[4] Michael E. Jones, Monsters from the Id: The Rise of Horror in Fiction and Film (Dallas: Spence Publishing, 2000).
[5] Jones, 66–100.

suffering represents the repression of emotions or humanity that modern science and reason demand. This scientist "monster" is a powerful moral critique of the dangers of science without moral restraint and can be seen in such movies as *The Boys from Brazil, Blade Runner, The Island of Dr. Moreau, Hollow Man, The Island, Turistas,* and *The Jacket.*

Another example of the Frankenstein monster motif is the serial killer, who becomes the evil yet rational extension of evolutionary survival ethics, as in *Collateral*; or the amoral monster created by a society that rejects the notion of sin, as in *Se7en*; or the beast that is justified by humanistic theories of behaviorism, as in *Primal Fear* and *Silence of the Lambs.* In *From Hell,* an investigating criminologist explains to an inspector that Jack the Ripper was probably an educated man with medical knowledge. The inspector replies with shocked incredulity that no rational or educated man could possibly engage in such barbaric behavior. All these serial killer films make the point that humanistic and Enlightenment beliefs about man's basic goodness blind us to the reality of evil.

Enlightened modern man has another weakness: the inability to deal with real supernatural evil. Because he believes that there is a natural scientific explanation for all spiritual phenomena, he is blinded to the truth of a spiritual dimension to reality. The classic example of this is *The Exorcist,* where a little girl possessed by a demon is analyzed by medical and psychological doctors. All of them seek natural explanations that remain inadequate because their worldview blinds them to the truth. This blindness to the supernatural is updated in the horror films *The Exorcism of Emily Rose, The Last Exorcism,* and *Paranormal Activity.*

The Reaping carries that naturalistic ignorance to new heights when a small southern town is being besieged by supernatural phenomena replicating the ten plagues of Egypt. A Christian apostate professor, who specializes in debunking paranormal phenomena, seeks to give natural scientific explanations for each plague, only to be confronted with true demonic spiritual reality. Her faith is restored in God when she experiences a supernatural arrival of God in judgment on the evil.

Social Commentary

Lastly, the horror and thriller genres can be effective social commentaries on the sins of society. Many Christians claim that we should not tell stories that focus on the evils of sin. They appeal to verses such as Ephesians 5:12: "It is disgraceful even to speak of the things which are done by [the sons of disobedience] in secret." I write about this "hear no evil, see no evil, speak no evil" interpretation in my newly updated and expanded edition of *Hollywood Worldviews: Watching Films with Wisdom and Discernment.* These critics read this Bible verse, and others, to teach that we should not speak of, let alone watch, acts of depravity in movies. But look at the verses before and after this "disgraceful to speak" verse. Ephesians 5:11: "Do not participate in the unfruitful deeds of darkness, but instead *even expose them.*" Ephesians 5:13: "But all things become visible *when they are exposed* by the light, for everything that becomes visible is light."

Paul is not telling us to *avoid* revealing deeds of darkness because of their disgracefulness; rather, he is telling us to *expose* them by talking about them. By bringing that which is disgracefully hidden out into the light, we show it for what it really is. This proper Biblical use of shame aids us in the pursuit of godliness.

This is exactly the tactic God uses with His prophets under both Old and New Covenants. God uses horrific explicit images in order to put up a mirror to cultures of social injustice and spiritual defilement. God used gang rape of a harlot and dismemberment of her body as a metaphor of Israel's spiritual apostasy (Ezek. 16, 23), and the resurrection of skeletal remains as a symbol for the restoration of His people within the covenant (Ezek. 37). Our holy, loving, kind, and good God also used the following horror images to visually depict cultural decay and social injustice: skinning bodies and cannibalism (Mic. 3:1–3), Frankenstein replacement of necrotic body parts (Ezek. 11:19), cannibalism (Ezek. 36:13–14; Psa. 27:2; Prov. 30:14; Jer. 19:9; Zech. 11:9), vampirism (2 Sam. 23:17; Rev. 16:6), cannibals and vampires together (Ezek. 39:18–19), rotting flesh (Lam. 3:4; 4:8; Psa. 31:9–10; 38:2–8; Ezek. 24:3, 33:10; Zech. 14:12), buckets of blood across the land (Ezek. 9:9, 22:2–4), man-eating beasts devouring people and flesh (Ezek. 19:1-8; 22:25, 27; 29:3; Dan. 7:5; Jer. 50:17), crushing and trampling bodies and grinding faces (Amos 4:1; 8:4; Isa. 3:15), and bloody murdering hands (Isa. 1:15, 59:3; Mic. 7:2–3). Horror is a strongly Biblical medium for God's social commentary.

Invasion of the Body Snatchers is a story that has had many movie remakes, with all of them reflecting the current cultural fears of each era. The basic template is a story about an epidemic of alien life forms coming to Earth and replacing human bodies with people who look the same but are part of a conspiracy to take over the planet. The original (1956) was a political analogy of the Red Scare of communist infiltration of the United States in the 1950s. The 1978 remake, starring Donald Sutherland, was a parallel to the 1970s conformity to the herd mentality of the New Age "me decade." *Body Snatchers* was the 1993 version that analogized the doppelganger takeover to a monolithic conformism to U.S. "military industrial complex," with a touch of AIDS paranoia thrown in. In 2007, *The Invasion*, with Nicole Kidman, became a parable of cultural imperialism and the postmodern "other."

Strong social criticism has been leveled by horror movies at various relevant issues in our culture. In *Underworld*, racism is paralleled and condemned through an "inter-species" romance between a werewolf and a vampire; *The Wicker Man*, damns neo-pagan Gaia religion in its murderous matriarchal colony of goddess-worshipping, man-abusing feminists. In one segment entitled "Dumplings" in the movie *Three Extremes*, abortion is likened to the sci-fi quest for eternal youth through cannibalizing our offspring.

One common theme in some horror movies is the degeneration of society into a selfish survival of the fittest ethic that animalizes us, versus a Christian ethic of self-sacrifice that humanizes us. In a sense it becomes a cinematic dialectic of the evolutionary worldview versus the Christian worldview.

28 Days Later is about Jack, who awakens in a hospital bed to discover all of London is empty of people — except for roaming zombies seeking human flesh. The zombies are the result of a viral contagion that sends people into a murderous rage. When Jack stumbles upon a fortress of military survivors besieged by the zombies, this isolated human society degenerates into its own animalistic survival. It is a parable of how untamed male aggression can become an evil culture of "zombies within."

In the sequel, *28 Weeks Later*, a father struggles with the moral guilt of saving himself at the expense of his wife's life when escaping from the zombies. He finds it hard to face his own surviving children later. The entire movie is an incarnation of the ethic of survival versus the ethic of sacrifice, the first making us no different than a zombie, the other making us human. Those in the movie who try to save themselves tend to end up stricken; those who try to rescue others at risk to themselves demonstrate the potential nobility of the human race.

This is not unlike God's own metaphor usage of zombie flesh eating to depict the depravity to which Israel's leaders had sunk in rejecting Yahweh's law:

> Mic. 3:1-3
> And I said, "Hear now, heads of Jacob And rulers of the house of Israel. Is it not for you to know justice? "You who hate good and love evil, Who tear off their skin from them And their flesh from their bones, And who eat the flesh of my people, Strip off their skin from them, Break their bones, And chop them up as for the pot And as meat in a kettle."

I Am Legend is a parable of a lone survivor, Neville, maintaining his humanity in the face of wild flesh-eating zombies. It becomes a Christ parable as Neville's blood contains the antibody to the viral contagion that caused the zombies in the first place. As a Christ figure, Neville must sacrifice himself to save others, but only after struggling with his doubts about God's goodness in light of all the evil. A fellow survivor's unwavering faith that "God has a plan" wraps up this movie that wrestles with God's sovereignty and evil, the primal instinct for survival, and the values of religion, sacrifice, and atonement.

30 Days of Night portrays vampires as metaphors for an atheistic evolutionary survival of the fittest ethic. When one victim whispers a prayer to God for help, the head vampire stops, repeats the word, "God," looks all around the heavens to see if He will answer, and then replies very simply, "No God" before devouring her.

It is important to remember that in a story, the worldview that the villain holds is the worldview that the storyteller is criticizing. So the fact that the vampires in this movie are atheistic, inhuman predators without mercy is a metaphor for the consequences of evolutionary ethics not a support of it. In contrast with this ethic, the people who do battle with them can only win by being more human, which is through altruistic sacrifice of themselves for others. Much like Christ taking on sin, the hero in this movie deliberately allows himself to be bitten and become a vampire in order to defeat the monsters before dying.

Discerning Good From Evil in Good and Evil

Horror and thriller movies are two powerful apologetic means of arguing against the moral relativism of our postmodern society. Not only can they reinforce the Biblical doctrine of the basic evil nature in humanity, but they can personify profound arguments of the kind of destructive evil that results when society affirms the Enlightenment worldview of scientism and sexual and political liberation. Of course, this is not to suggest that *all* horror movies are morally acceptable. In fact, I would argue that many of them have degenerated into immoral exaltation of sex, violence, and death. But abuse of a genre does not negate the proper use of that genre.

It would be vain to try to justify the unhealthy obsession that some people have with the dark side, especially in their movie viewing habits. Too much focus on the bad news will dilute the power that the Good News has on an individual. Too much fascination with the nature and effects of sin can impede one's growth in salvation. So, the defense of horror and thriller movies in principle should not be misconstrued to be a justification for *all* horror and thriller movies in practice. It is the mature Christian who, because of practice, has his senses trained to discern good and evil in a fallen world (Heb. 5:14). It is the mature Christian who, like the apostle Paul, can explore and study his pagan culture and draw out the good from the bad in order to interact redemptively with that culture.

CHAPTER 8: FREE DIGITAL BOOK

GET THIS FREE DIGITAL BOOK!
For a Limited Time Only

FREE

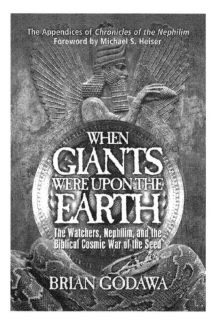

Biblical Research on the Watchers, the Nephilim & God's Cosmic War of the Seed!

By Brian Godawa

Chapters Include:
- The Book of Enoch
- Sons of God
- The Nephilim
- Leviathan
- Cosmic Geography in the Bible
- Gilgamesh and the Bible
- Mythical Monsters in the Bible
- Goliath was Not Alone
- Jesus and the Cosmic War
- AND MORE!

Click Here to Get Your Free Book!

www.godawa.com/free-giants-book

GREAT OFFERS BY BRIAN GODAWA

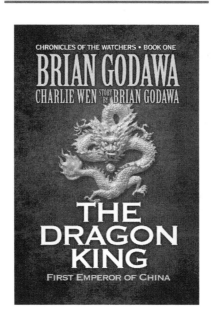

VIDEO LECTURES

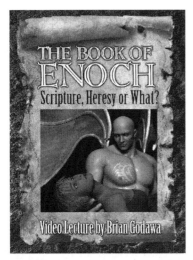

The Book of Enoch: Scripture, Heresy or What?

This lecture by Brian Godawa will be an introduction to the ancient book of 1Enoch, its content, its history, its affirmation in the New Testament, and its acceptance and rejection by the Christian Church. What is the Book of Enoch? Where did it come from? Why isn't it in the Bible? How does the Book of Enoch compare with the Bible?

Available on video and audio.

Chronicles of the Nephilim: The Ancient Biblical Story

Watchers, Nephilim, and the Divine Council of the Sons of God. In this dvd video lecture, Brian Godawa explores the Scriptures behind this transformative storyline that inspired his best-selling Biblical novel series Chronicles of the Nephilim.

Available on video and audio.

To download these lectures and other books and products by Brian Godawa, just go to the STORE at:

www.Godawa.com

THE IMAGINATION OF GOD

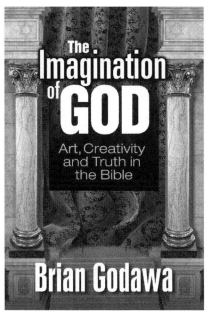

Art, Creativity and Truth in the Bible

In his refreshing and challenging book, Godawa helps you break free from the spiritual suffocation of heady faith. Without negating the importance of reason and doctrine, Godawa challenges you to move from understanding the Bible "literally" to "literarily" by exploring the poetry, parables and metaphors found in God's Word. Weaving historical insight, pop culture and personal narrative throughout, Godawa reveals the importance God places on imagination and creativity in the Scriptures, and provides a Biblical foundation for Christians to pursue imagination, beauty, wonder and mystery in their faith.

This book was previously released with the title, *Word Pictures: Knowing God Through Story and Imagination.*

Endorsements:

"Brian Godawa is that rare breed—a philosopher/artist—who opens our eyes to the aesthetic dimension of spirituality. Cogently argued and fun to read, Godawa shows convincingly that God interacts with us as whole persons, not only through didactic teaching but also through metaphor, symbol, and sacrament."

— Nancy R. Pearcey,
Author, *Total Truth: Liberating Christianity from its Cultural Captivity*

"A spirited and balanced defense of the imagination as a potential conveyer of truth. There is a lot of good literary theory in the book, as well as an autobiographical story line. The thoroughness of research makes the book a triumph of scholarship as well."

— Leland Ryken, Clyde S. Kilby Professor of English, Wheaton College, Illinois
Author, *The Christian Imagination: The Practice of Faith in Literature & Writing.*

For More Info
www.Godawa.com

How to Watch Films with Wisdom and Discernment
Amazing Video Lectures with Powerpoint and Film Clips!

Brian Godawa, Hollywood screenwriter and best-selling novelist, explores the power of storytelling in movies and in the Bible.

You will learn how storytelling incarnates meaning, worldview and redemption in movies.

You will discover the nature of subversion, and how narratives compete and win in the culture wars of both movies and the Bible.

You'll receive a Biblical foundation for understanding sex, violence and profanity in movies and storytelling.

Surprisingly, you will discover the 4 ways that horror is used redemptively in the Bible and in movies.

To learn more about this online course go to the STORE at:

www.Godawa.com

ABOUT THE AUTHOR

Brian Godawa is the screenwriter for the award-winning feature film, *To End All Wars,* starring Kiefer Sutherland. It was awarded the Commander in Chief Medal of Service, Honor and Pride by the Veterans of Foreign Wars, won the first Heartland Film Festival by storm, and showcased the Cannes Film Festival Cinema for Peace.

He also co-wrote *Alleged*, starring Brian Dennehy as Clarence Darrow and Fred Thompson as William Jennings Bryan. He previously adapted to film the best-selling supernatural thriller novel *The Visitation* by author Frank Peretti for Ralph Winter (*X-Men, Wolverine*), and wrote and directed *Wall of Separation,* a PBS documentary, and *Lines That Divide*, a documentary on stem cell research.

Mr. Godawa's scripts have won multiple awards in respected screenplay competitions, and his articles on movies and philosophy have been published around the world. He has traveled around the United States teaching on movies, worldviews, and culture to colleges, churches and community groups.

His popular book, *Hollywood Worldviews: Watching Films with Wisdom and Discernment* (InterVarsity Press) is used as a textbook in schools around the country. His novel series, the saga *Chronicles of the Nephilim* is in the Top 10 of Biblical Fiction on Amazon and is an imaginative retelling of Biblical stories of the Nephilim giants, the secret plan of the fallen Watchers, and the War of the Seed of the Serpent with the Seed of Eve. The sequel series, *Chronicles of the Apocalypse* tells the story of the Apostle John's book of Revelation, and *Chronicles of the Watchers* recounts true history through the Watcher paradigm.

Find out more about his other books, lecture tapes and dvds for sale at his website **www.godawa.com**.